Make the Internet Your Warm Market
The Complete Guide to Networking through Instant Messaging

Max Steingart

Make the Internet Your Warm Market

The Complete Guide to Networking through Instant Messaging

By Max Steingart

For general information on our other products and services please contact our Customer Service Department - info@maxsteingart.com

Printed in the United States of America

ISBN: 0-9767271-0-2

Published by Success Online Publishing
300 South Pointe Drive - Suite 2206
Miami Beach, FL 33139

www.MaxSteingart.com
info@MaxSteingart.com

"In the land of the blind, the one-eyed man is king."

Dedication

This book is dedicated to the millions of innovative, entrepreneurial men and women around the world who have opened their eyes to a new way to conduct business. They blend technology with passion in the high-tech, high-touch pursuit of success.

Make the Internet Your Warm Market

Table of Contents

Foreword

With the dawn of the Internet and computer technology you now have at your fingertips a vast pool of prospects worldwide to help you become successful. But if you don't know how to get to them and cause those people to warm up to you this immense pool of potential customers and friends might as well not exist.

How can you find them and then turn them into a Warm Market that can greatly improve your bottom line? The answers are in this great book by Max Steingart.

A Warm Market is vital to the growth and profitability of any company. It is central to the income of all sales people marketing their products or services. In the business world, marketing is one of the most fundamental things you must become proficient at, and selling to a Warm Market is far better than to a cold market.

In this easy and fun-to-read book, Max shows you how to use the Internet and Instant Messaging to tap into this enormous pool of Internet users and instantly turn them into a Warm Market that is open to hearing about what you have to offer.

Everyone's Warm Market is limited unless you learn how to tap into the Internet. There you will have an unlimited supply of people you can turn in to warm prospects right at your finger tips.

With the valuable information that Max provides in this wonderful book, you can also make new friends around the world-not just temporary friendships that are here today, gone tomorrow, but friendships that are strong and rewarding.

You remember the popular idea of pen pals? What Max teaches takes that idea into the 21st century and beyond. People are not only using it to increase business, they are using it to make new friends and have fun.

Networking is the best way to get a job. It is the best way to get leads. It is the best way to find out about just about anything that is important to you from sources that you can trust. Networking on the Internet is an established practice. It is now mainstream on a worldwide basis, but only Max makes it fun and easy.

This book is the complete guide to creating a delicious Warm Market through networking with Instant Messaging on the Internet. It should be required reading for everyone in sales or anyone looking for new customers. That covers just about every business and sales person on the planet. It provides an easy-to-understand road map of the Internet highway. You won't get lost with this map.

Instant Messaging is the most popular way people communicate with others on the Internet. There are nearly 250 million* people around the world that use Instant Messaging to reach out and touch someone. Imagine communicating with any one of them without picking up the telephone.

If you have wanted to start using the Internet to create more business or want to do it better, but don't know how, Max Steingart's book will be a Godsend to you. If you want to maximize your ability to increase your customer base and profits through a Warm Market then knowing how to use the Internet and Instant Messaging are essential. With this book Max has made it easy and fun to do.

Jack M. Zufelt
Author of the #1 best selling book
The DNA of Success and Mentor To Millions
www.dnaofsuccess.com

---

* at time of printing

Notes to the reader

This book has been written to help you fully utilize one of the most powerful aspects of the Internet, the direct connection that Instant Messaging provides to millions of people. Instant Messaging is having a major impact on every Internet user's life and on every kind of business.

If you asked anyone that was successful in business what the fundamental basis for their success was, they would answer you with one word. RELATIONSHIPS.

Relationships have always been at the foundation of success in every kind of business. People do business with, and refer business to people they like and trust. You wouldn't buy insurance, make a financial investment, purchase a home, or go into a business venture with someone you didn't like or trust.

The Online process for establishing a relationship or friendship with someone new and having them become customers or clients goes like this:

- **You make a new friend**
- **Your new friend learns what you do**
- **Your new friend wants what you're selling**
- **You repeat the process**

This book shows you how to make a new friend on the Internet with an Instant Message. The rest of the Online process occurs as a natural part of the developing relationship with your new friend.

You must establish an Online friendship with someone before you talk to them about your business. A person has to like you and trust you before they will be interested in what you do or sell.

Today, millions of people are using Instant Messaging (abbreviated IM) and the Internet to begin new relationships with total strangers because it's convenient and provides many worthwhile advantages. They also use Instant Messaging to maintain relationships with the people that they know.

The Internet stories you read in this book are all based on actual people and events. Some of the stories are based on my own personal experiences. The names and Screen Names used in this book have been changed. Any similarity between Screen Names mentioned in this book and existing Screen Names used on the Internet today is entirely coincidental.

If you're involved in any kind of business (i.e. sales, executive recruiting, insurance, real estate, financial services and investments, etc.) where networking with people is an integral part of your business, you can use Instant Messaging to make new friends and establish relationships with people that will become your new clients and new customers.

This book shows you why the Internet is the perfect place for making new friends and establishing new business relationships. This book provides you with the tools, strategies, and tactics to connect with the best people. Effective use of Instant Messaging enables you to establish an immediate relationship with anyone.

Instant Messaging is an invaluable tool you can use to communicate with people when you use it properly.

Sending out Instant Messages to strangers with a blatant sales pitch or link to a web site is called SPIMMING. It is not acceptable behavior, nor is it effective. It is the Instant Message equivalent of email SPAM. SPIMMING is not a smart thing to do. It will get you into trouble and not produce the results you want. In many places it's also against the law.

This guide was prepared to show you how to use Instant Messaging effectively and productively.

Acknowledgements

My heartfelt thanks go out to the thousands of men and women who shared their Online experiences, emailed their stories, asked questions, pointed me in the right direction, and continuously encouraged me to complete this book.

Introduction

Are you ready to look at something new?

**Not now!! I don't have time to look at something new!!
Can't you see I've got a battle to fight!!**

In 1975, as a yacht broker trying to get the attention of the yacht brokerage industry, I mailed a postcard with this cartoon to three hundred companies. I was introducing a small computer system that would help other yacht brokers keep track of boats that were for sale.

Most people are resistant to change and initially the yacht brokerage community wasn't any different. After all, yacht brokers had a paper and manual filing system that had worked for years and they saw no reason to make any changes. They didn't know what a computer could do. That was then. Today, every yacht brokerage firm in the world uses a computer and elements of a system I helped to create.

If you're not using Instant Messaging and the Internet to help you in your business today, this cartoon is as relevant to you as it was to every yacht broker that received it in 1975.

Instant Messaging systems have a Buddy List to show you when the people you know are Online. They also have a Member Directory that provides you with amazing personal details about millions of other users you don't know. Initially adopted by the technologically adventurous, Instant Messaging has become accepted by mainstream society and should be used by everyone in any business.

I urge you to read this book carefully and look at the advantages Instant Messaging is bringing to millions of people.

Gerald's story

Gerald was a very successful businessman who lived in Seattle, Washington. He worked with a small group of local entrepreneurs. His company made and distributed health and nutritional products and he was interested in expanding his network to other parts of the country.

Gerald's company was hosting a meeting in Orlando, Florida in February – three weeks away. He was looking forward to attending the event because his company was introducing a new line of products there and he was anxious to learn about them. Gerald was eager to trade the cold, rainy, Seattle winter weather for a few days in the warm Florida sunshine. He was a terrific golfer and planned to take his golf clubs.

Early one January morning, he couldn't sleep and found himself searching on the Internet for a list of golf courses in the Orlando area.

While reviewing his search results for golf courses, Gerald decided to look for other golfers that might be Online.

It was 3:00 AM in Seattle and 6:00 AM in Orlando when Gerald met Lou Online. Lou was an executive vice president of sales in a company that manufactured paint products. He was Online, reviewing his stock portfolio before leaving for his office. Lou was also an avid golfer.

Gerald sent Lou an Instant Message:

LivingMyDream:

> **Hello, My name is Gerald. I see that you play golf. My handicap is a 7, what's yours?**

LS45962:

> **Good morning, I have a 7 handicap too. What are you doing up so early or late? I see you're in Seattle.**

LivingMyDream:

> **That's right, I live in Seattle, but I'm coming to Orlando in three weeks for a company conference. I'm planning on bringing my golf clubs and wanted to play some golf. I did a search on the net and have a big list of golf courses there. Can you recommend any good courses to play?**

LS45962:

> **I'm a member of the finest country club in Orlando with the best course. When exactly are you coming to town? Perhaps you can join two of my friends and I in a game? That is if you're really a 7 handicap. We all play on the same level.**

Gerald played golf with Lou on two of the days he was in Orlando. They learned a great deal about each other on the golf course. Lou learned all about Gerald's business and lifestyle. And Gerald discovered that after fifteen years of selling paint products, Lou was anxious to try something new. He was tired of selling paint and trying to beat last year's sales figures.

Lou liked the sound of Gerald's business. Lou was a fabulous salesman and convinced Gerald that he was just the man to help expand his network to the east coast.

Gerald was smiling as he walked to the terminal to catch his return flight to Seattle. He waved good bye to Lou who had graciously offered to take him to the airport.

Once again he had successfully met a new friend over the Internet that would help him expand his business.

The days of walking into a room full of strangers to network and develop friendships and business relationships with other people are winding down. Now, it's easier to meet someone on the Internet from the comfort of your home or office. You can do it on your computer with the click of your mouse. You can meet some wonderful people and make some great friends.

Think of the Internet as a very large room filled with strangers. Many of the people in the room are walking around with signs on their backs telling you all about them and encouraging you to talk to them.

Simply by reading the sign, you know each person's name, the city and state they live in, their marital status, and the number of children or grandchildren they have. Additionally, you know what they do for a living, their hobbies, and all the things they are interested in doing and talking about.

You can walk behind everyone in the room, read everyone's sign, and contact the people that indicate they have similar interests. You can know all about someone before you start a conversation. You can identify the people that share your work experience, your passion for a particular subject or hobby, and talk to only the people that have things in common with you.

Naturally, you wouldn't bother to talk to anyone in the room whose sign you didn't find appealing.

I'm sure you realize the incredible value of knowing all about someone before you talk to them. If you know enough about a person prior to talking to them, you can decide whether you want to talk to them or not.

In this book I will show you how to recognize a new "friend in the making" simply by reading the sign on their back.

I want to clarify that when I ask you to think of the Internet as one big room, I am NOT talking about Internet Chat Rooms. You'll find a detailed explanation of where you can meet people, in Chapter 5.

To gain admission to the room I describe you'll need to do a few things, including creating your own sign telling everyone in the room all about yourself. The other people in the room wearing signs on their backs are there to talk to and meet NEW people. That's the object of posting your information and interests on your sign in the first place.

Moving freely around the room you'll meet many people who will enjoy meeting you.

Millions of people are using the Internet and Instant Messaging to make new friends, create new business relationships, and maintain existing ones. This is the first book ever written that outlines the basic process of networking successfully Online.

This book directs you to the best places on the Internet to communicate with other people. It provides you with the three vital steps you need to take to reach more of the right people with an Instant Message. You'll find the entire process will save you time and money. And it's fun to do!!

New opportunities and people you never knew existed are available to you with just a click of your mouse.

I hope you enjoy this process as much as I have.

You're going to find this book invaluable if:

- You are always looking for new customers
- You want a simple way to meet new people and make new friends
- You want to learn how to establish a business relationship with anyone over the Internet
- Your success in business depends on talking to other people
- You don't want to talk to your friends about your business
- You're frustrated by making 'cold calls' to long lists of leads with few or no results
- You want to improve your Online networking skills

CHAPTER 1

What is your Warm Market and how can the Internet replace it?

Two weeks after I started a new business, Frank, the person that introduced the business to me, came to my home to explain how the business worked.

Frank asked me to make a list of all the people that I knew and all the people I had a relationship with. I was to list my family, friends, neighbors, and the people that I worked with and did business with. He called this list my "Warm Market."

I had never heard the term before even though I was familiar with the concept.

Trying to do business with people that know you has always been easier than trying to do business with strangers. The upscale department store, Nordstrom, would reasonably expect greater success from a promotional mailing to a list of their existing customers than they would get from a random mailing to a list of people in a specific zip code that were unfamiliar with the store.

When Frank handed me a phone script and told me to call everyone on my Warm Market list and tell them about our new business he was following a procedure that has been the mainstay for success in many types of business. Word of mouth recommendations can be very effective.

Traditionally, that's the way many businesses work – you tell the people that you know, they tell the people that they know, and so on and so on.

Why you want to go to your Warm Market

- You know a lot of people
- It is always easier to talk to someone that you know than it is to talk to strangers
- People are more likely to consider things recommended by their friends
- The people in your Warm Market like you. What you say to them has more credibility than when they hear the exact same thing from a stranger.

Potentially, your Warm Market would appear to be the first place to go when you're looking for new customers or starting any kind of business. But sometimes, it isn't always so.

Why you DON'T want to go to your Warm Market

- You don't want to sell to your friends
- You're not going to recommend something you're not sure about
- You don't have any credibility with the people that you know
- You want to talk to your friends after you've achieved some success in the business

If you CAN'T or WON'T talk about your business to the people that you know, you have to talk to strangers.

Talking to strangers about your business exposes you to a great deal of rejection. The sales cliché, "you have to go through one hundred no's to get a yes" is familiar to everyone in sales.

Like a lot of people, I didn't want to talk about my new business with the people that I knew for a number of reasons. I've always been very passionate and enthusiastic about everything I do. But initially, I didn't know enough about the new company I was involved with, or the industry itself, to feel good about recommending it to my friends. I found it easier talking to strangers about my business than talking to the people that I knew. So I ignored my Warm Market completely and looked for new people to talk to.

The "Three Foot Rule" in business is, If there is a person that's breathing within three feet of you, they're a prospect for your business.

The first seven months of my new career, like anyone without a prospect list, I lived the Three Foot Rule. I would talk to strangers wherever I would find them. I would meet people at Chamber of Commerce functions, at social events, at the mall, standing in line at the supermarket, at art shows, and at the marina where I kept my sailboat.

I would sit in the center seat of an airplane whenever I flew so I would have two people to talk to during the flight. For seven months, I even networked "Happy Hour" at two upscale bars on Palm Beach and signed up a large group of dysfunctional customers.

■

There's a NEW Three Foot Rule in business – *When you're sitting in front of your computer, you're within three feet of the entire Online world.*

■

I ran ads in newspapers for five months to get customers. I spent thousands of dollars advertising, with minimal results.

At the end of my first year in business I had one hundred and fifty customers. This number would grow to thousands of people in the second and third year of my business, as a direct result of the Internet and the example set by my friend Karla.

Karla's story

Karla, one of the few normal people I met at "Happy Hour," told me that she was going to buy a computer so she could meet people to talk to about our business and products.

I was skeptical. I laughed at her and suggested that she get psychiatric help. "It's easy to meet people," I told her.

It was easy for me to meet people when I was out and about, but it wasn't easy for her.

Two weeks after she went Online to meet people, Karla called me. She said, "Tomorrow, I'm going to the home of someone I met on the Internet to talk about our business and products."

I was concerned about Karla's safety. I cautioned her about the potential dangers of meeting strange people Online. She agreed to call me fifteen minutes after arriving at her new Online friend's home. If I didn't hear from her, I promised to call out the National Guard.

When my phone rang the day of the meeting, the man on the other end of the line was Karla's new Internet friend, Doug. He wanted to assure me that Karla had arrived and was perfectly safe. Doug told me that he was very interested in getting involved with our business.

Doug turned out to be an amazing and accomplished individual. He had been very successful in the automotive industry and had retired to a large riverfront estate. He had two computers connected to the Internet all the time. Doug told me, "I've made many great friends on the Internet. After all, I met you two. Didn't I?"

Doug knew a great deal about our business. Unlike me, he was quite comfortable talking to his friends about it. After filling out his application form, Doug told some of his friends about his newest venture on the telephone. He signed up eighteen new customers. For Doug, going to his Warm Market was easy.

I was so impressed that Karla could meet someone like Doug on the Internet that I went out and purchased my own computer. I figured if she could do it, I could do it too. Who wouldn't want to meet someone like Doug?

In the following 21 months my customer base would grow to thousands of people as a result of the relationships I developed and the wonderful friends I made on the Internet.

I never did go to my Warm Market. I made the Internet my Warm Market and used Instant Messaging to create new friendships and to find new customers. Upon closer examination, you will find that you can do the same thing.

Why the Internet can become your Warm Market

- You can dramatically increase the number of people you know using Instant Messaging

- Talking to someone new Online is as easy as talking to your best friend

- You can make a new friend Online in seconds and have immediate authority and credibility with them

- Your new Internet friends will like you and trust you. You are not a stranger. What you say to them has more credibility than when they hear the exact same thing from a stranger.

CHAPTER 2

Why I named this book
Make the Internet Your Warm Market

I've written this book to give everyone that would normally turn to their Warm Market for business prospects and customers an easy alternative. The Internet can replace your Warm Market.

This book outlines the process of how to use Instant Messaging to make new friends that will be interested in learning more about you and your product, service or business. The process worked for me, it worked for all the people I've written about, and it's working for millions of others as you're reading this.

If you follow the process you can eliminate the two biggest challenges you face when getting started in your new business; finding people to talk to about your business and dealing with the rejection that comes from talking to people that you don't know.

Why the Internet can replace your Warm Market

1. Convenience
2. Direct access to more people
3. People are easier to approach
4. Rejection is eliminated
5. Targeting is easier
6. It's more fun

Convenience

You can send an Instant Message to someone any time it's convenient. Morning, afternoon or evening, you can chose from millions of people that are Online at the same time you are. You're free to contact any of them when you know where to find them and how to use Instant Messaging.

You don't have to leave your home or office. You don't have to worry about what you're going to wear or if you're having a bad hair day.

Direct access to more people

Every day, you can connect with millions of people on the Internet. Long distance and time zones cease to exist when you use Instant Messaging. You can meet people, virtually, that live across town from you that you would never meet otherwise, and make a new friend with a simple Instant Message.

You can meet someone Online and establish a business relationship anywhere in the world, and you don't need a passport to do it.

People are easier to approach

Sending an Instant Message to someone Online is an easy way to connect with a stranger. On the Internet, the Screen Name and Profile you create position you to be immediately liked by anyone you contact. They provide enough information about you so you're not a stranger. If you contact people that share your hobbies, interests or personal values, they will respond. It's like your computer is directly attached to their computer.

Let's face it, people like talking to people with similar interests, or that are in the same line of work. Don't you?

Rejection is eliminated

Rejection disappears on the Internet because you know a great deal about someone prior to sending them an Instant Message. Everything they've written about themselves in their Profile is your open invitation to contact them.

The Internet Profiles of people clearly indicate who you want to talk to and who you want to avoid. You can identify people that are ambitious or lazy, and positive or negative, based on their choice of Screen Name and the content of their Internet Profile. You can recognize the people that will be interested in what you do by reading their Profile.

Instead of going through the traditional rejection numbers when you approach a stranger in person, you'll find that eight out of the ten people you contact with an Instant Message will be agreeable to looking at your business.

Targeting is easier

Whomever you prefer talking to about your business (doctors, teachers, stay at home moms or people in any type of profession), it's easier to find them Online and communicate with them in an Instant Message than it is to walk into a room full of strangers. There are Member Directories Online that let you search for people that have specific words in their Internet Profile so you can target the best people to talk to. You can actually find and talk to a physician Online easier than you can by trying to make an appointment to see him in his office. It's also easier to find people that share your passion for a hobby. You can make a new friend by sending a simple Instant Message.

It's more fun

Communicating with someone in an Instant Message is fun. Chatting with someone that shares common interests with you is enjoyable and can be rewarding. You choose who you want to connect with. You choose when you want to connect with someone. You have plenty of time to think about what you're going to say when you respond to someone's Instant Message.

The Internet is a very social place when you know how and where to find someone to talk to.

Oliver's story

Upon graduating from an Ivy League college Oliver was invited to join a prestigious stock brokerage firm on Wall Street because of his family's connections and the size of his personal stock portfolio. He was expected to bring in four new accounts each month and generate a specific level of business. He watched his fellow brokers hammering people on the telephone for new business and thought of a better way.

Oliver had used Instant Messaging since high school to communicate with his family and friends. When he went off to college, he found Instant Messaging kept him in constant touch with almost everyone he knew.

After Oliver contacted all his relatives with an offer to manage a portion of their stock portfolios, he turned to the Internet and Instant Messaging to find new clients.

Oliver searched Online for people who graduated from his university. He found that most of the alumni he contacted Online were very receptive to hearing from him.

His initial Instant Message to initiate a relationship with an alumnus was:

WallStreetWiz:

> **Hello, My name is Oliver. I'm a Harvard graduate with a degree in economics, working on Wall Street. What did you major in while you were there?**

The first six months of his stockbrokerage career, Oliver brought more new clients into his firm than any other new broker as a result of his innovative use of Instant Messaging.

The Internet can replace your Warm Market and provide you with an inexhaustible supply of new people to connect with. You'll be amazed at the thousands of wonderful people that are Online at any moment that share your interests, values, and experiences who are waiting to hear from you. You can make a new friend with a single Instant Message.

The Internet has already changed the dating scene with millions of singles turning to dating and matchmaking web sites every month. Internet-savvy people have learned that they can use the virtual world to contact a stranger Online with an Instant Message and establish a friendship and a business relationship in a few seconds. Millions of people are doing it right now as you're reading this.

Once a virtual relationship has been established with someone, it's easy to move it to the telephone and then to a face to face meeting, if and when it's appropriate.

CHAPTER 3

Why you want to use Instant Messaging

What is Instant Messaging?

Instant Messaging is a convenient way to see when your friends and family are Online and to communicate with them in real time. It's faster than email and more convenient than picking up the telephone. Many people use Instant Messaging to communicate with people that they work and do business with.

Sally:

> **Don't forget it's Henry's birthday tomorrow.**

Betty:

> **Gee Thanks, I almost forgot**

Instant Messaging is a type of Online communication system. It enables you to create a kind of private Chat Room with another individual in order to communicate in real time over the Internet. It is similar to a telephone conversation but uses text-based, not voice-based, communication. The message you type and send to someone instantly appears in a little box or window on their computer for them to read. They respond to your message and their reply appears on your computer screen. Typically, most Instant Messaging systems alert you whenever somebody on your private list of friends (Buddy List, Messenger List or Contact List) is Online. You can then initiate a chat session with that particular individual or they can contact you.

Hundreds of millions of people use Instant Messaging to communicate with their family members, friends, neighbors, co-workers, and business contacts. In short, people are using Instant Messaging to communicate with people in their Warm Market. Your Instant Message Buddy List tells you when anyone on the list is Online and they know you're Online too.

Instead of picking up the telephone, you can send an Instant Message to anyone. Long distance and time zones disappear when you use Instant Messaging. You can send an Instant Message to someone on the next block, in the next state, or on another continent. PC World Magazine projects that by 2006, business people will make up nearly half of the 506 million Instant Message users.

It has been reported that in the next two years Instant Messaging will surpass email as the primary Online communication tool. Almost half of the Online population currently uses Instant Messaging once a week, and a group of "intense" users has six or more conversations a day.

Instant Messaging use is growing, with more than seven billion Instant Messages being sent every day worldwide. There are nearly 250 million* people across the globe – and nearly 80 million Americans – who regularly use Instant Messaging as a quick and convenient communication tool.

Sending an Instant Message to someone you know has become a very popular way of staying in touch. Sending an Instant Message to someone you don't know can be the beginning of a wonderful friendship and business relationship or it can be viewed as an unwelcome intrusion.

How your Instant Message is received by a total stranger depends on the contents of your initial message. You want your initial Instant Message to be the start of a friendship, not a slick commercial for your business.

---

* at time of printing

One evening at a party in San Francisco, the subject of meeting people on the Internet came up in casual conversation. The host of the party was fascinated when I mentioned that a person could use a computer as a business building tool for prospecting and finding new customers for any business.

On a whim, we went into his home office and turned on the computer. I signed onto the Internet and did a search on two words: professional and Dallas. I wanted to see who was Online in Dallas that I could send an Instant Message to that had the word professional in their Profile.

There were 93 people Online at that particular moment that matched my search criteria. I selected one Profile out of the group and sent her an Instant Message. The following conversation made a believer out of my host and everyone else at the party.

Jill Masters

Member Name:	**Jill**
Location:	**Dallas, TX area (Ya'll)**
Sex:	**Female**
Marital Status:	**Married**
Hobbies:	**Love the outdoors (even in this heat) Let's go to the lake !!!**
Computers:	**desktop and laptop**
Occupation:	**Professional**
Personal Quote:	**Smile...it has a nice effect on other people :-)**

Mentor2006:
> **Hello, My name is Max. I'm 52. How old are you?**

JillMasters:
> **Hi, Max. My name is Jill. I am 36 Nice to meet you!**

Mentor2006: | **I write and teach what do you do?**

JillMasters: | **I am a radiology tech**

Mentor2006: | **do you glow in the dark? LOL**

JillMasters: | **nah, just a myth...lol**

Mentor2006: | **glad to hear that**
how long have you been doing that, it sounds like fun?

JillMasters: | **just over 5 years. where do you live?**

Mentor2006: | **I live in Palm Beach, Florida but spend time in Dallas. I have business interests there**
I'm in San Francisco today on a friend's computer so I'm making all kinds of typo's

JillMasters: | **that's neat**

Mentor2006: | **I'll be back in Dallas on Friday**

JillMasters: | **I have been in Dallas most of my life**

Mentor2006: | **I like it there I have a lot of friends there too!**

JillMasters: | **me too, it is where I call home**

Mentor2006: | **I teach people how to run a business from their home on their computer. This is a fascinating medium don't you think?**

JillMasters: | I think so, that sounds great to me

Mentor2006: | the entire world is moving on to the Internet

JillMasters: | very true
I would love to be able to do that

Mentor2006: | love to be able to do what?

JillMasters: | have an income generating business on my computer

Mentor2006: | are you really serious?

JillMasters: | yes, very serious
what kinds of businesses do you teach about?

Mentor2006: | do you like working with people?

JillMasters: | of course...I work with my patients every day
I am a people person
very outgoing

Mentor2006: | tell you what, will you be Online later?
I'm here in San Francisco for a party, I'm actually in the middle of it and they just started serving my favorite appetizer. (pigs in a blanket) I signed on to the Internet to prove a point

JillMasters:	**what kind of business are you talking about?**
Mentor2006:	**I'll email you the web site for the business and we can talk later**
JillMasters:	**I am supposed to go shopping in a few minutes with a friend...to get a maid of honor dress for her wedding** **I will be home after that**
Mentor2006:	**great. I'll look for you later**
JillMasters:	**Nice to meet you!!**
Mentor2006:	**nice to meet you too, it looks like I have a new friend in Dallas!! :)** **see you later**
JillMasters:	**Yes you do and thank you, I'm glad you found me**
JillMasters:	**bye for now have fun at the party**

You have to talk to people if you want to be successful

Let's face it. If you're trying to make a living in a business and need new clients or customers, Instant Messaging is your ticket to success.

You can talk to someone new every time you turn your computer on. Throw the old Three Foot Rule out the window with yesterday's vinyl records.

Barney's story

Barney had achieved a level of success in his company that was rarely attained. He was one of the legends of his industry. He did business all around the world and his monthly income was in the mid six figure range.

Barney had been using email for years and had some limited experience using Instant Messaging with his Warm Market. He knew about Buddy Lists and Address Books but he never paid any attention to the Member Directory in his Instant Messaging system. He didn't know he could use a Profile as a magnet to attract people to him or use it to make him likeable and credible to everyone Online.

After listening to a set of my Internet training CDs, Barney's Internet adventure really began. After creating his Screen Name and posting a Profile in the Member Directory, he started to contact people.

Barney was amazed at how easy it was to find someone to respond to his Instant Message. It became an amusing mind game as he looked at people's Profiles. He wanted to come up with an opening line that the recipient couldn't possibly ignore if they saw it. He read each Profile looking for the creator's hot button and made reference to it in his initial Instant Message.

Barney found that half the people he sent an Instant Message to would answer. He wasn't the most accurate typist or the fastest typist but it didn't seem to matter. Most of the time, the people that answered him typed as badly as he did.

Time flies when you're having fun

Sometimes, after an extended Online type fest, either Barney or his new Online friend would suggest moving their conversation to the phone to speed things up.

The amount of time he could spend Online talking to someone interesting really surprised Barney. Time would fly by. He felt it was time well spent.

After using Instant Messaging to meet new people for a week, Barney called me. He said, "Every time I walk by my computer I know there is someone Online that I could be talking to and it excites me. I do business with people all around the world at odd hours. Yet every time I'm Online I connect with another awesome person. I didn't sleep for the first two nights."

You should be using Instant Messaging to communicate with the important people in your Warm Market.

Suggest to your friends that they download the same Instant Messaging system you're on or ask what they use. Don't act surprised when you find out most of them already use one. Share your Screen Name and email address with them and ask for theirs.

You will find that staying in touch with your Warm Market is easy. Add everyone to your Buddy List and you will see them when they're Online. Add everyone to your address book so you can send them an email with a click of your mouse.

You'll be amazed at how much more productive and attentive you'll be when you use Instant Messaging with everyone.

Effective Instant Messaging eliminates rejection

Talking to strangers is not an easy thing for most people to do. When you start talking to strangers in the hopes of acquiring a new client or customer, rejection becomes an unavoidable part of the situation. And while no one likes to be rejected, successful salespeople have learned to accept rejection as a part of the sales process.

You're not a stranger to anyone when you have a Screen Name and Profile. Everyone you contact will warm up to you instantly if they like the Screen Name and Profile you create.

Obsolete sales clichés thanks to Instant Messaging

- You have to go through one hundred <u>no's</u> to get a <u>yes</u>
- People aren't rejecting you; they're rejecting your product
- Don't take rejection personally, you're not the message, you're the messenger

You can contact people based on your own criteria when you use Instant Messaging. You can prejudge people with amazing accuracy because they provide so much information about themselves in their Profile.

You can read between the lines of any Profile and pick someone that you would enjoy talking to, knowing that they would probably feel the same way.

- You won't waste time, you'll have fun
- You won't be rejected, you'll be embraced
- You won't waste money, you'll make more money

Instant Messaging systems and their Member Directories make locating and contacting the best people an easy process.

- You're only going to contact or respond to people you know you'll like so personal rejection is not an issue
- You're only going to contact or respond to people that like you so personal rejection is eliminated
- You're only going to contact or respond to people that will most likely be interested in what you do so you don't waste time talking to the wrong people. And you won't have to deal with rejection

Prospecting for new friends and customers can be a fishing expedition

The charm of fishing is that it is the pursuit of what is elusive but attainable...a perpetual series of occasions for hope. Each person you talk to could be your next best friend, next customer, or client.

Just as the oceans are filled with fish, there are millions of people on the Internet, and many of them would be interested in what you're doing or offering. You simply have to find them and send them an Instant Message.

The Instant Messaging systems discussed in this book have two features you are going to find invaluable: A Buddy List that makes you aware of when the people you know are online so you can communicate with them; and, a Member Directory that provides you with detailed information about the other users of the system.

⚠ WARNING

Instant Messaging is fun, can be habit forming 😊 and may be addictive.

CHAPTER 4

The value of the Member Directory

Most Instant Messaging systems have Member Directories that permit each user to publish personal information that can be read by everyone else using the system. These directories were created to give people an opportunity to make new contacts and new friends.

People that use an Instant Messaging system to communicate with just their friends don't use the Member Directory. They don't fill out an Online Profile because their friends know who they are and they don't want to be contacted by strangers.

The Member Directory is just like the telephone book where everyone has the option of listing their telephone number or having an unlisted number. Only instead of a one-line listing, with your name, address and telephone number, the Member Directory gives each person a chance to publish extensive details. When someone takes the time to publish a personal Profile in the directory, the words they use indicate their Online agenda, what they are interested in and what they like to talk about. The more details someone provides in their Profile, the more open they are to hearing from strangers.

The more interesting your Profile appears to others, the more it will attract people that search the Member Directory looking for someone to talk to. The more appealing your Profile is to other people you contact, the better your response will be.

The Member Directories are primarily used by people looking to meet new people, to make new friends, and to create business relationships. Each directory has search features attached to it that will permit you to sort through the millions of Online Profiles and find those matching your own unique searching criteria. You can find people with similar interests and experience by looking for Profiles that contain the same words you use in your Profile. Someone searching the Member Directory can find you the same way.

In addition to being able to find a Profile of someone that shares your interests, most Member Directories permit you to specify that the person is Online and logged into the Instant Messaging system while you're doing your search.

Instead of rushing to the Chamber of Commerce business card exchange to meet new people, you can sign onto any Instant Messaging system, search the directory and connect with someone that is Online when you are. Each Instant Messaging system is a community of millions of users that are open to meeting new people and making new friends.

Using an Instant Messaging system is like walking into the world's biggest room where millions of people have poster-sized signs on their backs.

Having this kind of information about a stranger before you start to talk to them is a dream come true for anyone in business. It's invaluable information.

It's easy and a lot of fun to walk around the room or search the directory and read what everyone has written about themselves. You can identify the people you will enjoy talking to based on what they've written in their Profile. You can identify the best people to approach as easily as you can pick a green M&M out of a bowl of mixed candy.

Screen Name

Each sign or Profile is labeled, <u>All about Me.</u> Printed on each sign, or personal Profile, is the following information about each person:

- Their first name
- The city and state they live in
- Their marital status - you know if they are married, single, widowed or divorced
- How many children and grandchildren they have
- A list of their hobbies and all the things they like to do and like to talk about
- A description of their occupation and work related experiences
- All kinds of additional personal information about them that will tell you if they are ambitious or lazy; if they are positive or negative about life

You can approach and talk to people that share your interest in a hobby, your work experience, or your passion for any particular subject. People like talking to people that like the same things that they do. People enjoy meeting people that have similar or common interests. Don't you?

Richard's story

When Richard started using Instant Messaging to meet new people he never had a problem finding someone in the Member Directory to talk to. His problem was getting someone to answer his initial Instant Message.

Richard sold an insurance package that many companies liked to provide to their employees as an extra incentive or perk. His ideal contact in any company was the owner of the company, the CEO, the president, or the director of human resources.

Richard's searches in the Member Directory for Profiles containing the words business owner, CEO, president, director, or human resources resulted in hundreds of matches.

Everyone reading his Screen Name and Profile could see he was active, accomplished, and interesting to talk to, yet no one responded to Richard's initial Instant Message.

Richard called me to express his frustration and I agreed to help him. While both of us were on the telephone and Online at the same time, we searched the Member Directory using his search criteria.

He pointed out the Profiles of the people he wanted to contact. He was picking good ones. It wasn't until I took a good look at Richard's Profile that I immediately identified his problem.

No, there was nothing wrong with Richard's Profile. His problem was that he had nothing of a personal nature in common with any of the people he was trying to contact.

Richard's Profile indicated he was interested in Bible study and participated in many church activities.

I suggested that he modify his search criteria of business owner, CEO, president, director, or human resources to include the words Bible study and church.

When Richard searched with the newer parameters he once again had hundreds of matches. Each matching Profile indicated the person shared Richard's interests in the Bible or their church as well as being someone that would also be interested in what he was promoting.

I could hear the enthusiasm rise in Richard's voice on the phone as he looked at the Profiles produced by his amended search. Not only could he identify and relate to all of these people, but he knew he would enjoy talking to them too.

Richard called me a few days later to thank me again. He had made twelve new friends and landed three new accounts using Instant Messaging.

Identifying the best people to talk to Online or in a room full of strangers is easy if you know all about them before you say "Hello." Thanks to the Member Directory and Instant Messaging, you can do exactly that.

You'll feel like you're attending a twenty-four hour worldwide party when you take advantage of any or all of the numerous Instant Messaging systems on the Internet.

CHAPTER 5

The best Instant Messaging systems

Each Instant Messaging system is a separate party with millions of people attending. It's easy and fun to have an Instant Message conversation with someone.

The four largest Instant Messaging systems listed below will give you free direct access to millions of people. (listed in order of number of users)

Yahoo	www.yahoo.com
ICQ	www.icq.com
MSN	www.msn.com
AOL	www.aol.com

(See Appendix A for complete details on all of the web sites and Instant Messaging systems listed in this chapter.)

While there are many other Instant Messaging systems available, you'll have your hands full working with these four free ones.

There are also Internet communities that use Instant Messaging and charge small monthly subscription fees to access the other people connected to their community. Monster.com, class reunion sites, and Internet dating sites traditionally charge their users.

Monster.com	www.monster.com
Class Reunion	www.reunion.com

Classmates.com	www.classmates.com
Match.com	www.match.com
Matchmaker.com	www.matchmaker.com

You can use any Internet Search Engine to find the most current list of Instant Messaging systems, as new ones become available all the time. (See Appendix A for a list of the most popular Search Engines.)

Most Instant Messaging systems don't interface with each other, and it will be necessary to log on separately to each Instant Messaging network to communicate with its members.

There are some software programs available that permit you to merge several Instant Messaging systems and Buddy Lists together. (A list is provided in Appendix A.)

Each of the Instant Messaging systems listed offers unique features. It's highly advisable to familiarize yourself with Yahoo, ICQ, MSN or AOL before you make a heavy investment in advertising for prospects or in a lead-generation campaign.

The Member Directory in any Instant Messaging system makes finding the best people to talk to as easy as picking a cashew out of a bowl of mixed nuts.

CHAPTER 6

The first step to making a new friend

Create a Screen Name

The first action you're required to take when signing up for any Instant Messaging system is to set up an account and create your "Screen Name."

A Screen Name identifies you to everyone you send an Instant Message to. It's your Internet Call Sign. Most people use some variation of their birth name or nickname when they set up their Screen Name or email address.

Your Screen Name appears before the @ in the email address you're assigned when initially joining an Internet community or Instant Messaging system, i.e., Screen_Name@yahoo.com.

BillSmith@yahoo.com, MaryJohnson@aol.com or MJ2255@msn.com are examples of the typical Screen Names you'll encounter.

Using your birth name as your Screen Name will certainly help identify you to the people that you know, but it doesn't help you very much when trying to contact someone that you don't know.

It's easy to identify the new Internet users by their Screen Name because they let the Instant Messaging system create them, resulting in a Screen Name of random numbers; e.g.: 15998876@yahoo.com or 87499955@aol.com

Some telephone company ISPs routinely use the first four letters of the user's last name and the last four digits of their phone number to set up their Screen Name. John Smith would be Smit4508@bellsouth.net. Mary Jones would be Jon22 11@attnet.net. After a brief period Online people usually create a new Screen Name that gives others an easier way to identify them and remember who they are.

Create a Screen Name to accomplish three things

1. Attract people to you
2. Make people curious about who you are and what you do
3. Make people like you

The Screen Name you create will make it easy to make a new Online friend. It acts like a magnet and attracts people to you on the Internet and helps lower any barriers of resistance someone might have in responding to your Instant Message. Your Screen Name is an important part of your virtual identity and an open invitation for others to contact you. Screen Names will make people curious about who you are and what you do.

TheLifestyleCoach	TheMillionaireMaker
TheMentor4Health	TheSuccessCoach
ThePoolsideDiva	BettyAtTheBeach
TravelingMary	MovingUpTony
TheHappyCamper	LuckyLarry

One of the easiest ways to promote what you do to others is to promote it in your Screen Name. Screen Names in this next group imply an involvement in the stock market in some way. Anyone interested in stocks, bonds, or investments would be more inclined to contact someone or respond to an Instant Message from someone with a very descriptive Screen Name.

WallSteetGuru   TheStockWiz
MissWallSteet   InvestmentQueen

People searching a Member Directory that are looking to network with someone that can help them buy or sell any type of property would be more likely to contact or respond to someone with a creative and interesting Screen Name. Screen Names like these will get you more attention than a nondescript name.

TheLifestyleRealtor   TheLotMaven
TheRealEstateMan   RealEstate911
Denise4RealEstate   TownhouseGuru

There are many names that focus on an occupation or business, such as:

Doctors – DoctorGoodSkin, SkinDoc2010, DrSkinHelper, DoctorGoodTeeth, DrMakeWell, DrFeelGood

Lawyers – LarryTheLawyer, RightsProtector, TheTicketFixer, TheLitigator,TheAdvocate

Sales – MrBenefits, InsuranceMan, AnnuityKing, MrWorkFromHome, FashCash4You, TheAvonLadyinTX, WeightLossMentor, ShakleeForYou, MrWallStreet, TheMeatMan

Do you have a hobby or interest you're passionate about? You may have more fun using a Screen Name that focuses on your hobby instead of your occupation.

Bowling	MrTenPin, TheStrikeKing,
Golf	MrAvidGolfer, NancyTheGolfer,
Tennis	MrTennis, BaselineBobbie, TheTennisAce,
Skiing	DownHillRacer, SnowBunny86,
Sailing	CaptainMike, MrSailorMan, GreatFirstMate,
Skating	MissBlades, SkatingGal.

People that are Online and open to making a new friend or hearing from a stranger are more likely to respond to an Instant Message from someone with an interesting Screen Name than from someone with a nondescript one. This also applies to personal Profiles mentioned in the next section.

TheSuccessMaker	InsightfulMary
BlondAmbition	SuzySkyDiver

A good Screen Name will set the tone for the kind of conversation you have with anyone. A person must be interested in you before you can expect them to be interested in your business or what you're selling.

One of my students wrote to me about her initial Instant Messaging experience:

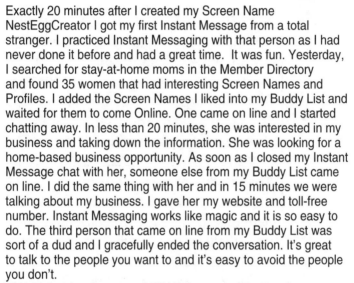

From: NestEggCreator
To: YourOnlineMentor

Hi Max,

Exactly 20 minutes after I created my Screen Name NestEggCreator I got my first Instant Message from a total stranger. I practiced Instant Messaging with that person as I had never done it before and had a great time. It was fun. Yesterday, I searched for stay-at-home moms in the Member Directory and found 35 women that had interesting Screen Names and Profiles. I added the Screen Names I liked into my Buddy List and waited for them to come Online. One came on line and I started chatting away. In less than 20 minutes, she was interested in my business and taking down the information. She was looking for a home-based business opportunity. As soon as I closed my Instant Message chat with her, someone else from my Buddy List came on line. I did the same thing with her and in 15 minutes we were talking about my business. I gave her my website and toll-free number. Instant Messaging works like magic and it is so easy to do. The third person that came on line from my Buddy List was sort of a dud and I gracefully ended the conversation. It's great to talk to the people you want to and it's easy to avoid the people you don't.
Thanks for showing me a GREAT way to market.

Debra Schooler

Mary Anne's story

Mary Anne relocated from Macon, Georgia to Orlando, Florida and started a career in real estate. As the proverbial new kid on the block in her company, she had a lot to learn about the area and the housing market there.

Mary Anne used Instant Messaging to communicate with her friends and family back in Macon. She created the Screen Name, TheRESpecialist, in the hopes that she might connect with people searching the Member Directory looking for a home or a realtor.

One evening she received an Instant message from a stranger.

MovingToFlorida:
> **Hello, my husband and I are looking to buy some vacant lots in your area as investments.**
> **Are you familiar with what is available?**

TheREspecialist:
> **Hello, yes I am. My husband and I have purchased a few lots ourselves as investments. I'm very familiar with the market and would be happy to point you in the direction of some great buys.**
> **My name is Mary Anne. What's yours? By the way, I like your Profile.**

MovingToFlorida:
> **Thank you, my name is Jean. My husband's name is Murray. I liked your Profile too. That's why I contacted you. We'll be coming down there in a week. Can you give me a call tomorrow so we can set up some time to look at some property with you?**

TheREspecialist:
> **Of course. When is the best time to call?**

Jean became Mary Anne's best client. Jean and Murray had recently cashed out of the stock market with millions to invest in property. In the following sixty days they purchased enough real estate with Mary Anne to make her the top sales person in her company for the entire year.

Create a Screen Name that will make people curious

The Screen Name you create will become one of the focal points of almost every Instant Message conversation you have with a stranger. People will be curious as to why you came up with the name. The words used in a Screen Name usually indicate something the person wants to talk about. In many cases the Screen Name reveals a person's Online agenda. You can start an Instant Message with anyone by asking a question about their choice of Screen Name.

More of Karla's story

Karla, the postal worker I talked about in Chapter One, lived in a small town. She really didn't like working at the post office. Her goal was to make enough money in her part time business so she could quit her full-time job. She wanted to spend more time riding her horse.

Having recently moved from New Jersey to Florida, Karla didn't know anyone in town. She didn't have a Warm Market. In fact, the only people she knew in Florida were her fellow co-workers at the post office and no one there wanted to hear about her new business.

She'd heard from other people in her company that they were using Instant Messaging on the Internet to make new friends and establish new business relationships. A few of the people she talked to about business networking on a computer said they were also using it to find dates. Karla knew that if other people could find someone Online to talk to about their business, she could too. She purchased a computer for the sole purpose of using it to meet people.

Karla learned very quickly that her choice of Screen Name would influence the content of her Instant Message conversations.

Karla's first Screen Name was KS33407. Her initials were KS and her zip code was 33407. Whenever she had an Instant Message conversation, the person always asked about her Screen Name.

> *"Why KS33407?"*
> *"What did KS33407 represent?"*
> *"What was the significance of the number 33407?"*

These questions became a predictable part of every Instant Message conversation Karla had.

When Karla changed her Screen Name to TheCynergistUSA, people still asked questions about her name.

> *"Why TheCynergistUSA?"*
> *"What did TheCynergist mean?"*

Karla's answers to these questions made people curious and interested in learning more about what she did.

> *Synergy is a combined action or operation between people that is mutually advantageous to all the parties involved. I enjoy connecting successful people in the USA together in an enterprise that changes their lives. I really like what I do*

was her answer every time someone questioned her choice of Screen Name.

It's possible to create and use more than one Screen Name. A Screen Name like CoachForHealth would encourage people to talk to you about health issues. The Screen Name CoachForWealth would invite conversations of an economic or lifestyle nature. People contacting the WeightLossCoach would most likely be interested in losing weight.

When Karla created another Screen Name, SuccessGal2005, the nature of her Instant Message conversations changed. She was routinely asked:

> *"What do you do?"*
> *"What made you so successful?"*
> *"Could you help me become successful?"*

Create a Screen Name that will make people like you

Donna's story

Donna was a young woman that was married to a soldier stationed in Iraq. She was living in Louisiana near the military base her husband's unit originated from. Donna sold cosmetics and juggled raising two young children with her business activities. She was always trying to find additional customers but her children came first. They kept her busy and she didn't have much private time to socialize and network to meet new people.

Donna wanted to use the Internet to find new customers because it was convenient and gave her access to other women. She could meet people Online without leaving her home. She signed onto Yahoo and created the Screen Name TheLifestyleChanger.

Within five seconds of logging on to Yahoo's Instant Messenger, she received an Instant Message from a man in her area who liked her Screen Name.

BayouBob:

> **Hello, I like your Screen Name.**
> **What do you do?**

This was a question she would be asked over and over again. Donna responded with an answer that she would use repeatedly every time the same question came up.

TheLifestyleChanger:

> **Hello. I work with other women. I show them how to create an additional income stream working from home that dramatically changes their lifestyle. Would you know any women that might be interested in something like this?**

BayouBob:

> **As a matter of fact I do. Would you have some time later today to speak to my wife? She is looking for something to do from home.**

Twenty minutes later, Donna was on the phone with the couple talking about her business.

The first week Donna was logged into Yahoo she had eight people contact her after finding her Screen Name in the Member Directory. All of them were interested in learning more about what she did after a few minutes of conversation.

Your Screen Name can set the stage to begin a conversation about what you do

In 1996, when I first went Online, I wanted the Screen Name Mentor. Everyone wants a mentor. A mentor is someone that has been down the road you want to go. Mentors can save you a lot of time and provide short cuts because they have information that can make your situation easier. A mentor is a coach and a trusted friend. There are a lot of great things you can do with the word mentor, like MentorAlice, MikeTheMentor, GoodHealthMentor, TheSuccessMentor, etc.

I couldn't get the Screen Name Mentor – it was already taken. Every Screen Name in an Instant Messaging system must be unique just like every email address is unique. No two people can have the same Screen Name. After several unsuccessful attempts at securing the Screen Name I wanted, the system automatically offered an alternative Screen Name – Mentor2006 – that I settled for.

Every time I had an Instant message conversation with a stranger they would always ask me

> *"What is going to happen to me in the year 2006?"*
> *"Why was that number in my Screen Name?"*

The answer I responded with made people want to know more about me and what I did.

> *I'm working with a company that is creating a growing stream of residual income for me. By the year 2006, I expect my income to be large enough that I can be sailing in the South Pacific on a 150-foot sailboat with ten of my closest friends.*

My favorite responses to this Instant Message were:

> *"Can I be your friend?"*
> *"Is there room on the boat for me?"*
> *"Are there opportunities in my area to do what you do?"*

Additional Screen Name tips

If you like a particular Screen Name and it's already taken, you can add numbers or letters to the end of the name and make it unique.

If SuccessMaker isn't available, try SuccessMaker2010.
If TheDietCoach isn't available, try TheDietCoach4U.

Make it easy for someone to read your Screen Name

When creating a Screen Name composed of multiple words, capitalize the first letter of each word you use so that the words are easier for other people to read.

GeorgeTheMentor is easier to read than georgethementor.
OnTopOfTheHeap is easier to read than ontopoftheheap.

Screen Names make it easy to identify the people you don't want to talk to

As you search for people to talk to, you'll quickly learn who you want to talk to and who you want to pass by.

Screen Names like Hemlock4U, Poison Ivy, HeartBrokenInNJ, MiserableInManhatten, and BlondBabe4U are examples of names of people you may want to avoid.

CHAPTER 7

The second step to making a new friend

Post a Profile

The next step to establishing your Internet presence is to post your personal Profile in the Member Directory of the Instant Message systems you plan on using. Almost everyone you contact will check out your personal Profile before responding to your Instant Message. They are going to want to know who you are or a little about you before they answer.

A good Profile sets the stage for you to be immediately liked and respected even before your Instant Message conversation begins. Like your Screen Name, your Profile invites people to respond to your Instant Message when you send one, or it provides the incentive for people doing searches in the directory to contact you. The more you tell people about yourself in your Profile, the more you can expect to hear from others. The words you use in your Profile will attract people to you that are interested in those very words and subjects.

Create your Screen Name and Profile before you contact anyone so the person you contact will know as much about you, as you know about them from reading their Profile.

When you send someone an Instant Message, that person is going to look at your Profile before they respond to you. Your Profile gives you immediate credibility, likeability, and a history with the people you contact before your conversation begins.

The rules about Profiles on the Internet are:

- The words people put in their Profile indicate what they like to talk about
- The more people write about themselves, the more open they are to accepting an Instant Message from someone they don't know
- Do not post personal details about yourself that can identify you and be used to hurt you

Pick the best way to describe what you do

When I was growing up, Jackie Gleason had a very popular TV show called The Honeymooners. In the show, his character, Ralph Cramden, was a bus driver, and his best friend was Ed Norton, played by the comedian Art Carney.

Ralph always called Ed by his last name. Norton was a sewer worker who worked under the streets of New York City. Whenever anyone asked Norton what he did, his response was always, "I'm a Subterranean Engineer." You sure get a different mental image from the words "subterranean engineer" than you get from the words "sewer worker," don't you?

Norton wasn't lying about what he did. He just found a better way to describe what he did that made him more appealing and give him greater stature.

Choose the words you use in your Profile carefully because your words might be misinterpreted. Words have multiple meanings.

Nido Quibain tells an interesting story illustrating how words can be misunderstood. A man comes to America for the first time from a third world country, where most of the houses have dirt floors. The man can barely speak and read English.

The man arrives at the airport in Los Angeles after an 11 hour flight from his country. He leaves the plane in a hurry and is desperately in need of a bathroom. If you do any traveling, I'm sure you can relate to this story.

He starts to run down the terminal looking for a bathroom. He doesn't want to have an accident, but he feels like he's about to burst as he hurries past slower moving people.

And then he sees the sign he is looking for. The sign reads: **"For bathrooms use the stairs."**

How many different ways can he interpret that sign?

You need to be sensitive to how many different ways the words in your Profile can be interpreted.

There was an actual sign posted in a dry cleaner's window in Japan that read: **"Drop your trousers here for best results!"**

Roberta's story

Roberta in San Diego was interested in using Instant Messaging to find clients for her business. She created the Screen Name IdealForYou that featured the name of her company, Ideal Nutrition.

Every time she signed onto the Internet she received dozens of Instant Messages from single men in her area and from as far away as London. All of the men contacting her were looking for a date. The contacted her because her name implied that she was ideal for them.

The words you use will attract people to you

Listing the name of your company in your Profile can be a bad idea. You may want to keep some anonymity in your identity and Profile until you're sure you want to tell someone. When many people read a company name in a Profile, they assume the person is Online trying to sell them something and they won't answer an Instant Message.

It's better to say stockbroker than stockbroker at Merrill Lynch. Having the company name in your Profile could attract any unhappy customer of Merrill Lynch to bother you.

If you're in business for yourself, you can use words that give you more stature by referring to yourself as a business owner, entrepreneur, consultant, lifestyle coach, mentor, teacher, recruiter, trainer or lifestyle developer.

You can call yourself the CEO, President, Chief Operating Officer of your own company.

More and more women today are starting businesses out of their homes. The Internet affords them the opportunity to work from home while taking care of their children.

Anyone that is a mother would certainly want to have the word Mother in her Profile. Mothers wear many different hats. They are counselors, chauffeurs, gourmet cooks, relationship specialists, mediators, special event planners, investors, developers, bookkeepers, organizers, serious time jugglers, fantastic multi-taskers, and so much more.

A mother that listed many of these descriptive words in her Profile would receive Instant Messages from people that were interested in any of those topics..

Adding the words "event planner" would attract other event planners or people interested in talking to an event planner. You're not trying to sell a product or service with your Profile; you're trying to sell you.

When you look at other Profiles, you can easily identify the people that would be open to hearing from you because they fill their Profiles with details about who they are and what they like to talk about. As you look at other Profiles, if you see something someone has written that applies to you, you can always add it to your Profile. A Profile, like you, is a work in progress that can be improved and changed all the time.

The more people write about themselves, the more inclined they are to accept an Instant Message from someone they don't know

If someone doesn't want to be contacted by strangers, they don't fill out a Profile in a Member Directory. The directory is for Profiles of people who want to meet new people.

Don't waste your time trying to contact people with minimal information in their Profiles. They won't be as open to hearing from you or as talkative as someone that fills in a complete Profile.

You'll get much better results if you send an Instant Message to someone that gives you lots of details in his or her Profile. The more information you can read about people in their Profile the better decision you can make about whether or not to contact them. When people with a sketchy or brief Profile contact you, try to learn more about them by asking direct questions. Their answers will tell you if you want to continue your conversation.

If a person's Profile doesn't list what he or she does, it's a safe bet the person either doesn't like, or doesn't want to spend time on the Internet talking about what he or she does.

Be specific when creating your Profile

To make your Profile more appealing and motivate people to respond to or contact you, avoid general descriptions and use specific words to describe who you are and what you like to do. Remember that people search focusing on specific words.

Vague words	Specific words
Outdoor activities	mountain climbing; whitewater rafting; camping
Music	country western music; classical music
Doctor	dermatologist; plastic surgeon
Professional athlete	professional golfer; professional football player
Sales	stockbroker; real estate; insurance sales executive; director of marketing; VP of sales; executive recruiter

A good Profile makes it easy for someone to like you

Your Profile should make you appear to be a positive, friendly and upbeat person. You want to appear professional and avoid using words that may be misinterpreted or deemed inappropriate. Do not provide details of your personal appearance unless you're Online looking for a personal relationship or a date for Saturday night. That's what people do when they're Online looking for love.

From: ManhattanSkeptic
To: YourOnlineMentor

Max, how can I trust what people write about themselves in their profiles? How do I know they're telling the truth? I don't want to waste my time talking to the wrong people.

ManhattanSkeptic

From: YourOnlineMentor
To: ManhattanSkeptic

Take it from someone who has met people everywhere; people lie in face-to-face situations too. It's not hard to identify someone online that isn't being truthful. In fact, I think it's easier to identify a liar online. Time always promotes or exposes everyone. You won't spend as much time as you think with someone online before the truth comes out.

Your Online Mentor

From: JustMary
To: YourOnlineMentor

Dear Mentor

What if a person doesn't have any interesting hobbies or interests? I'm 55 yrs old. I retired 5 yrs ago and have been looking for part time business since then. All I did was raise my children and now helping with my grandchildren. I never really got into any hobbies or anything interesting. I watched my husband go to work ,come home, go to church and maybe visit friends and watch movies or go to the park with the kids. So you see, it was just a boring time for me then. Now that I've retired, I still don't have any hobbies. I guess what I'm trying to ask is: What would a person like me put in a profile that will not run other people away?

Thanks,
JustMary

From: YourOnlineMentor
To: JustMary

Dear JustMary,

You have a lot of things to talk about...and lots to
still do. Even if you consider the first half of your
life has been boring, it doesn't mean the rest has to
be. There are many things you could write about
in your profile.

You could mention: Your children, Your grandchildren
(grannies can talk ENDLESSLY about that!), Your
church, What kinds of movies do you like? Where
do you live? What did you retire from? What WOULD
you be interested in doing? - life isn't just about the
past, it's about what you want to do in the future.

You could find a lot of other middle aged women in
the same boat and form a "Bored old Grannies" Group
and start a chat room or a Blog. You could start by
 changing your screen name from JustMary to
MaryOnTheMove.

Your Online Mentor

Do not post personal details about yourself that can identify you and be used to hurt you

If you think there is good in everybody, you haven't met
everybody. A Profile in the Member Directory can be seen by
everyone. Don't provide personal details about yourself that can
be used against you. Don't list your last name, street address,
or phone number in your Profile. Your first name is all you
need to provide in a Profile. You want to use your Profile as a
screening mechanism to give people enough information about
yourself so they are interested in talking to you, but not enough
information that enables a person to initially identify where you

live. Your Profile is visible to everyone on the Internet. Don't share your personal contact information with someone until you're sure who you're talking to.

Don't list the name or location of the company you work for. You can provide that information to someone on a need-to-know basis, when you decide you're comfortable giving out the information.

CHAPTER 8

The third step to making a new friend

Contact someone

Contacting someone is your next step after you've created your eye-catching Screen Name and Profile. There are millions of people Online right now that are open to receiving an Instant Message from you.

Who are the best people for you to talk to?

That's something you have to decide. And you have a lot of choices – millions, in fact.

A creative Screen Name and Profile is a person's open invitation to be contacted. You can tell a great deal about a person's Online agenda by his or her choice of Screen Name and Profile.

BlondBabe4You may be Online looking for her soul mate or just a date for next Saturday night. The details of her Profile will tell you exactly what she likes to talk about and who she's looking for.

BrokenWingNJ may be Online telling the world she's hurting because she's getting a divorce or she's been dumped by her boyfriend. She could be at a low point in her life and her Profile would provide all the details. She wants to talk about her current situation and her problems.

You have much better choices of people to contact than either of these two.

You don't want to send out Instant Messages indiscriminately. Review the Screen Name and Profile of everyone before you send them an Instant message.

As you search for people to talk to, you're going to notice appealing and descriptive Screen Names (HappyMary, TheAntiqueQueen, etc.), traditional Screen Names (MikeSmith, MJJones, etc.), and Screen Names with no apparent meaning (4539884, 784906, etc.). No matter how much or little thought they've given to their Screen Names, most people manage to provide enough information about themselves in their Profile to help you determine if you really want to talk to them.

You want to avoid the obvious Screen Names of people with Online agendas you're not interested in. You would be better off talking to MovingUpMary or BlondAmbitionNYC than HeartBrokenTX.

Always look at a person's Profile before you talk to them and find something in it to comment about. Only contact people that have Profiles filled with information about themselves. There are so many people that have posted complete Profiles that would be open to hearing from you. Don't waste your time contacting people with sketchy or incomplete Profiles.

A person's Profile tells you a great deal about him or her. Does this person share your interests and values? Is this a positive person? Why do you think this person would be someone to contact about your product, service or business?

In 1998, I recorded my first set of Internet training tapes in a studio in Dallas, Texas. The technician operating the recording equipment and editing the material had listened to my lessons over a three-day period of time. On the fourth morning of taping he came into the studio with a big smile on his face. He told me that the previous night he went Online and created his own Screen Name and personal Profile. Then he did a search for someone that liked the same things that he did and made a new best friend in an hour. He couldn't believe how much fun it was to do, or how much he had in common with his new best buddy. You can experience the same thing. And you can do it over and over again. Every day, you can find as many new people Online to contact and talk to as you care to. The total number of people you contact each day is up to you. The more selective you are about who you contact and respond to, the greater your Online success will be.

Don't contact anyone unless you can say, "I really like your Profile. If you can't say it, keep scrolling down your search results until you find someone you can say it to.

- **Pick someone whom you would enjoy talking to that would appear to be a good prospect**
- **Pick someone who shares your passion for a particular hobby or subject**
- **Pick someone who has things in common with you**
- **Contact someone whose Profile provides plenty of details**
- **Contact someone whose Profile has a good positive personal quote**

Barbara's story

Barbara was a successful sales rep for a newspaper that started her own part-time nutrition business from home. She planned on attending a convention put on by the nutrition company in Salt Lake City. Over eight thousand people traveled there each year to hear the latest company announcements firsthand. The event reunited friends in the business from around the world and gave everyone there a chance to meet new people and learn the newest sales strategies that were working for others.

Three months before the event, Barbara went Online looking for people in the Salt Lake City area that she could Instant Message. She wanted to meet people there that were involved in sales. To be more specific, she was looking for successful sales people who were ambitious and dissatisfied with their current situation.

Barbara had been a top sales performer in her company for the last five years, but she wanted more. She wanted a stream of residual income that she knew she could make with her part-time business. She was looking for people that wanted more out of life than what they currently had. She wanted to meet people like herself.

Even the best salesperson has to deal with the reality that they are only as good as their last good month. Each year, the traditional sales cycle renews itself.

Barbara enjoyed talking to sales people and explaining the concept of residual income that made her business so appealing to her. Her goal was to meet eleven people in Salt Lake City using Instant Messaging. She quickly learned to identify who to talk to out of the thousands of people that were Online.

The Member Directory she used had a section in each Profile for a "personal quote." Barbara noticed that she had her best Instant Messaging conversations with people that had detailed Profiles and positive personal quotes. When Barbara contacted people without personal quotes or with quotes that were humorous but a bit negative, her Online conversations didn't turn out too well.

Positive personal quotes found in Profiles:

- Life's a dance...don't be a wallflower
- When you cease to dream, you cease to live
- Success is a state of mind
- What your mind can conceive and believe, your mind can achieve

Negative personal quotes found in Profiles:

- Sometimes you're the bug, sometimes you're the windshield
- Sometimes you're the pigeon, sometimes you're the statue
- Life is like a bowl of chocolate Exlax; you always know what you're going to get in the end
- Life is like a freeway and I'm always stuck in traffic

Each day Barbara would send the same Instant Message to sales people in Utah with a good Profile. Her Screen Name was BlondAmbition08.

BlondAmbition08: **"Hello, my name is Barbara. I'm coming to Salt Lake City for a convention in five weeks. Could you please tell me the name of the best place for steaks in Salt Lake City?"**

People would look at Barbara's Profile before responding to her Instant Message. Not only did she learn the names of the top three places for steak in Salt Lake City, she connected with eleven people that were all interested in meeting her while she was in town. Three of those people elected to sign up in Barbara's nutritional business before she arrived in Salt Lake.

Your success depends on the number of people you contact and who they know

Melanie's story

Melanie Rogers was a young woman living in a rural area in central Canada. She had been taking some nutritional products recommended by her chiropractor and decided she wanted to make a little extra money each month recommending them to other people.

Melanie didn't have a Warm Market to talk to about her business. Her chiropractor suggested that she mail out promotional audio tapes to a list of names she purchased every month. Each week for an entire year, she would mail out ten tapes to different people on the list. She soon developed a lottery ticket mentality toward each mailing. Every week she thought, "One of these people is going to listen to the tape and call me." But it never happened.

Melanie heard that other people in her company were using Instant Messaging to meet people Online to talk about their business. She attended a special Internet training I was doing at her company's fourth-quarter meeting in Chicago because she wanted to learn another way to find new customers. When she saw for herself how easy it was to meet new people on the Internet, she got excited.

When Melanie returned home from Chicago, she created the Screen Name MarvelousMelanie along with a fabulous Profile. Since she didn't have the ability to meet many people on a local level, she wanted to use the Internet to meet people in the cities where her company held promotional conventions. The company's next event was in Orlando, Florida, and Melanie planned to attend.

Melanie's opening Instant Message line to everyone she contacted in Orlando was:

MarvelousMelanie:

> **Hello, My name is Melanie. I'm coming to Orlando at the end of January for a convention. Do you know what the temperature will be there then?**
> **I'm in Canada and expect it will be 5 or 10 below zero here.**

Melanie made twenty new friends in the Orlando area with that initial Instant Message. Six of her friends signed up for her business prior to the convention and attended it with her. Before she left town, she signed up an additional six people.

The Internet and Instant Messaging made all the difference in Melanie's success

A year and a half later, when Melanie's company expanded their distribution of products into the United Kingdom, she immediately started making new friends in London. She started each Instant Message conversation with a compliment and a reference to the person's Profile.

MarvelousMelanie:

> **Hello, I like your Profile. I'm coming to London at the end of July for a five day convention. My company is expanding our business there. How difficult is it to get a tour of Buckingham Palace? And can you recommend any other sights to see while I'm there? I'd really appreciate your help.**

Melanie made six good friends in London this way and made plans to meet them all when she was there.

On her first day in London, Melanie met all of her new Internet friends. All of them signed up in her business. One of them was the head coach of a professional soccer team who was a local celebrity.

The coach convinced everyone connected with his team that they needed to be taking the company's products and signed them all up as customers. As a result, Melanie became her company's first national marketing director in the United Kingdom.

So, Melanie, a woman who didn't have any sales activity in her company the first year she was in business, found incredible success as a result of Instant Messaging. She also learned that who the people you talk to know is as important as the number of people you talk to.

From: MentorMike
To: YourOnlineMentor

Dear Mentor

Hi Max, I've been one of your students for two months. Now I have a problem: my buddy list is full! Max, I've exposed more people to my business opportunity in the last two months than I have in the last two years! I want to tell you one quick story. I'm going to call this person Joe. My initial chat with Joe was OK, but not great. I began sending him your daily motivations, but did not tell him about my business opportunity. (See Appendix E for information about Your Daily Motivation.) Joe had been a specialized airline mechanic for 20 years, but had been laid off post September 11th. My business opportunity has a nominal expense to get started, but to Joe, nominal might as well have been $1 million. I have no doubt that I found him at the lowest point in his life. Several days later, Joe sought me out and restarted our conversation. Since then, I have probably spent 10 hours chatting with Joe, almost always our conversation centers around the message in your daily motivation. To date, Joe has not joined my business opportunity, but here's the thing: he has referred three people to me, all three have joined my business opportunity, and over the last 30 days, they have been my three top producers! Max, my selfish side says don't tell anyone else, because I have truly found a gold mine in your training; but my compassionate side tells me your training should be shared with everyone who is looking for an opportunity. I thank you Max, and I am certain Joe thanks you.

Sincerely, Mike

CHAPTER 9

How to search for the right people

The Internet gives you the greatest chance to find the best people to talk to in the least amount of time. You can search a Member Directory for someone to Instant Message and have thousands of choices of people to contact that are Online at the same time you are. And all of your resulting matches will share your interests and values.

You can waste a lot of time looking at Profiles unless you learn how to search effectively.

The key to searching effectively and finding the right people is to select someone that has as many things in common with you as possible. You don't have to guess, "Is this someone I might be interested in?" You'll know when you read their Profile. Out of all your available choices, you want to contact the people that provide the most details about themselves in their Profiles.

> **You don't have to guess, "Is this someone I might be interested in?" You'll know when you read their Profile.**

It's important that you have an idea of who you're looking for before you begin to search.

Who do you feel the most comfortable talking to?

- Men or women?
- Would you prefer talking to someone that was married, single, divorced or a widow/widower?
- Do you want to meet someone that lives in your town or in another part of the country?
- Would you like to connect with someone overseas?
- Are you interested in talking to someone with a particular vocation or work experience?
- Would you like to contact someone that went to your alma mater?
- Would you prefer talking to someone that shares your interests in a hobby or a particular subject?

Each Member Directory has its own format for doing searches. As you familiarize yourself with several of the directories, you'll develop your personal favorites.

There are various ways to search through a directory

- Gender search – You can search through a directory by gender if you have a preference for talking to men or women
- Age Grouping search – Many Member Directories permit searches by age groups. For example, Yahoo gives the following age range search options: no range, 18-25, 25-35, 35-50, 50-70, 70+. It's more productive to include an age preference in your searches so you'll avoid looking at all the Profiles created by children

- Marital Status search – You can search for people based on the posted marital status in their personal Profile. The usual options and choices could be: single; married; long term relationship; single – not looking; single and looking; separated; divorced; widow/widower

- Location search – You can search for Profiles of people in your city, town, state, province or country. Or you could expand your search to anywhere in the world

- Key Word search – You can search for people that have particular key words in their Profile like camping, sailing, aerobics, horses, German Shepherds, exotic birds, travelling, movies, theater, fine dining, etc.

- Occupation search – You can search for people that have key words in their Profiles describing what they do for a living: lawyer, chiropractor, dentist, teacher, sales, holistic physician, office manager, nurse, executive assistant, etc.

- Hobbies and Interests Search – Your best search results will occur when you find Profiles containing the words of subjects that you are passionate about. You can search for people with the words: Bible, Jesus, Church, Scriptures, Christ, or Psalm 23. You can search for people that have personal quotes in their Profiles from your favorite authors or philosophers – Zig Ziglar, Anthony Robbins, Jim Rohn, Socrates, Plato, etc.

As you look at the Profile of someone you are contemplating contacting, it's important to look at the details they provide about themselves. Make it a rule only to contact people that have complete Profiles. The more information in the Profile, the more inclined the person will be to respond to your initial Instant Message.

Just because someone has the word teacher in their Profile doesn't mean that they're a teacher. The Profile could have been written by a ten year old child that writes, "I want to be an English teacher when I grow up." Or, it could have been written by an adult with serious personal issues that writes, "I hate teachers." Reading each Profile completely before you contact anyone will save you time and reduce the chance of contacting the wrong people.

The people that write the most in their Profile are inviting you to contact them

Avoid contacting people with sketchy, incomplete Profiles. Focus on contacting the people with Profiles that contain positive personal quotes. A Profile without a personal quote is incomplete.

Every search you do in a Member Directory can result in anywhere from thirty matches to several hundred.

Every time you do a search there will be new people to contact. If you did the same search every thirty minutes, the results would be different as people are continuously logging on and off the Internet.

"If I had an hour to spend chopping down a tree, I would spend 45 minutes sharpening my axe, and 15 minutes chopping down the tree."

Benjamin Franklin

Many directory searches limit their results to a specific number of Profiles. By changing a few parameters you can expand your search results beyond the limits of your original search to get different results. Each specific search will result in new unique matches.

For example, if your search to see who is Online in Tampa resulted in 100 matches, you can modify your search criteria and amend your search to include gender. If you search for men and women separately, you'll get 200 matches or 100 for each gender. Changing your search by adding other specific words will produce additional results.

The fastest way to target precisely who you're looking for in your search is to get very detailed. Indicate a specific occupation or hobby, a specific location, or search by your gender and marital status preference. You can do additional searches by looking in neighboring cities or you can search by indicating a state or country location. The broader your search parameters are, the more Profiles you'll have to look at to find someone suitable to contact.

When doing location searches, many directories list the cities and states for you. You simply have to highlight the area of your choice. Other directories ask you to type the location preference in yourself. In these situations, you're going to want to type them in two different ways so you'll see the most Profiles. You'll do a search by first spelling out the name of the state. Then search again and use the two letter postal code abbreviation. Searching each way will produce entirely different results. Example: Florida and FL; Texas and TX; California and CA, etc.

Your success in connecting with the right people is going to be based on the quality of the people you contact and talk to about your business, not the number of people. Remember, quality is better than quantity. You have to be selective about who you approach Online and spend your time with. Make sure you can say, "I'd like to talk to this person; I like their Profile."

The more time you spend reviewing Profiles before you contact someone, the more productive, fulfilling, and rewarding your Online conversations are going to be. The Internet provides you with an unlimited supply of people to talk to about your business.

Christine's story

Christine had been an executive secretary and administrative assistant for eleven years before she became a mother. She had planned to return to work after giving birth, but those plans changed when she gave birth to twin boys.

She was determined to remain home with them and devote herself to their education, personal growth, and development for as long as they needed her.

Christine's husband ran a successful business and they were doing alright financially, but the income from her previous job was missed.

When the boys turned five, Christine found that she had a few hours each day to devote to something. The question was what? A part-time job? Classes at the local college? A part time business that she could work from home?

Christine opted for finding a business that she could work from home. She had recently been introduced to a business that she could work from home by the mother of one her children's playmates. The business involved the sale of children's toys. She had already purchased a number of these toys for her own children and felt she could enthusiastically recommend them to other parents.

So Christine went into the toy business. She made a list of all the people she knew in the area that might be interested in some toys. She included her neighbors and the parents of her children's friends. She was going to invite some of the mothers to her home to check out the toys and would serve some light refreshments. When she began to contact the people on the list, she was disappointed to learn that most of her Warm Market had already been introduced to the toys by another mother in the area.

Christine was stumped without a Warm Market to turn to, until her sister suggested using the Internet. Christine had been using Instant Messaging to talk to her sister in Detroit and brother in San Jose for years. Her sister asked:

> *Why not use Instant Messaging to talk to other women who are home raising small children?*

Christine couldn't think of one reason why she couldn't. She signed up with three Instant Messaging systems. After creating her Screen Name and Profile in each system, she started contacting other mothers Online.

She felt she could talk enthusiastically to any other mother with small children, but she especially enjoyed talking to mothers with twins.

She searched each Member Directory with a very specific search criteria. She made her searches gender specific. She was clear on her marital status category. She wanted to contact only married women and she wanted women with twins.

Christine's opening Instant Message to everyone was,

> *Hello, My name is Christine. I've got twin boys age five. How old are your twins? Are they identical or fraternal?*

Christine's use of Instant Messaging and the Member Directories kept a constant flow of women coming to her home. She was very selective about who she Instant Messaged. She usually had several Online conversations and two phone conversations with everyone before extending an invitation to visit her home and see the quality of the toys she was selling.

Christine's use of Instant Messaging enabled her to develop a nice network of local women that she never would have had access to otherwise.

Once you find someone Online with a good Profile, the next step is to send them an Instant Message. The entire process can be fun and perfectly safe if you follow some simple rules.

From: ShockedBeyondBelief
To: YourOnlineMentor

Dear Max, Is it me, or was I the only normal person on the Internet the other night? Please allow me to clarify. I began searching for key words that I thought might indicate a common interest. First I tried words that might indicate openness to my company's products. I started with "aromatherapy" then "health" then "cancer prevention" and even tried things like "leadership" and "Online marketing." The results astonished me.

I may be a prude, but no matter what I used for a keyword search, the result was the same. Men and women using the Yahoo messenger service to sell their pornographic web sites. Even if you never click on the actual link to go to the site, the user IDs that they use are so ridiculously crude that I was embarrassed just looking at the screen. I kept plugging in different search word scenarios for over four hours. My conclusion is that I am not willing to encourage anyone that I care about to subject themselves to a community that clearly doesn't fit my profile for a business partner.

In fairness, I did not load the ICQ or AOL software. In your experience, would I find the same environment on ICQ and AOL?

I was definitely excited about your information and the amazing potential of reaching people around the corner and around the world. I am not willing to wade through the muck to get to them.

You are 110% right about everything else that you said about the process of searching for a new business partner.

Whether you meet the person face to face at the dry-cleaners or greet them on-line, the process is the same. You still have to say hello, develop rapport, ask great leading questions, determine their moral compass, show you care about them, qualify them for your enterprise, help them to identify their why, and encourage them to sell you on why you should invest the next five or ten years mentoring them. Once you have done all of this you may wish to offer them the opportunity to fulfill their potential as part of your business family.

The Internet is a vehicle. I readily admit that I am a novice concerning its potential. As you have gathered, my first foray into the world of Instant Messaging has left me not wanting to share the concept with anyone that I care about. Under no circumstances would I subject anyone on my team to the filth contained on the member's ID list.

Can we expect a different result from ICQ and AOL? If there is a way that I can see this concept working, I will get behind it 100%+ but for now I have even uninstalled the Yahoo software from my computer. Please share your thoughts and experience at your earliest convenience. Have a blessed day.

ShockedBeyondBelief

From YourOnlineMentor
To: ShockedBeyondBelief

Dear ShockedBeyondBelief

You didn't search properly and your search results exposed you to the dark side of the Internet. Rest assured, you can avoid the dark side completely. Searching for one or more words in a profile doesn't get the job done. You needed to be doing an advanced search that would enable you to add additional searching criteria.

The first time I searched the Member Directory I had the same experience. It wasn't until I learned an easy way to search effectively that my results changed. Initially I would have quit after reaching the same conclusion you did, but for one thing. You see, a good friend of mine used the member directory to connect with a very successful entrepreneur.

The Internet gives you access to everyone and as you discovered, that's not necessarily a good thing. You don't need or want to talk to everyone. You want to connect with people like yourself and completely avoid the people you mentioned, who have questionable Online agendas.

To search effectively you must target precisely the people you want to talk to. By doing so, you'll achieve different results than you experienced. The key to successful searching is to filter out all the bad, crazy profiles with questionable content and find only the good ones. It's a simple process when you know how.

Searching using one or two key words isn't enough to filter out the people you want to avoid. In addition to the key words searches you are doing, add any of the following words: church, bible, bible study, scriptures, Christ, Jesus, synagogue, Psalm 23 or other words of a spiritual nature and you will virtually eliminate the porn content.

Adding to your key word search the additional parameter of "married men and women" would have screened out some of the silliness too.

Your Online Mentor

The Internet rules for contacting the right people

Internet Rule # 1 Always listen to your inner voice when it comes to judging people. If you feel uneasy about someone during your Instant Message conversation or after talking on the phone, move on to someone else.

Internet Rule # 2 The people that write the most in their Profiles are inviting you to contact them.

Internet Rule # 3 The choice of words used in a Screen Name and Profile clearly indicate the person's Online agenda and what they want to talk about. If during your Instant Message conversation you don't like the tone or the direction, move on to talking to someone else.

Internet Rule #4 Know what you're not looking for. Many people have interesting Profiles but are Online looking for their soul mate or a date for Saturday night. These people post physical descriptions or anatomical details of how they look. Their Online agenda is 'love' and they may not be your best choice. If there is anything in a person's Profile that bothers you, move on to another.

Internet Rule #5 Know what you're looking for. You can find precisely who you're looking for by reading a person's Profile. In fact, you'll have more choices than you can imagine of wonderful people to contact.

Internet Rule #6   End your contact and conversation with anyone when it ceases to be fun or isn't going the way you want.

Internet Rule #7   Never invite someone you're meeting for the first time to your home unless you've had numerous phone conversations and feel completely at ease with them. It's safest to meet them in a public place (i.e., restaurant, shopping mall, hotel lobby),

List your favorite search parameters and key words describing your ideal contact.

1. _____

2. _____

3. _____

4. _____

5. _____

6. _____

7. _____

8. _____

9. _____

10. _____

11. _____

12. _____

CHAPTER 10

The Internet relationship game

Establishing a friendship Online that turns into a business relationship is like a baseball game. In baseball you start out at home plate. After you hit the ball, you have to get to first base, second base and then third base before you return back to home plate. Your ultimate goal is to get around all the bases and score a home run.

The Internet relationship game is the same, whether you're initially looking for a new friend, new client, new customer, or a date for Saturday night. You go through the same steps no matter what your Online agenda is. When it's appropriate, your conversation with someone will move from talking about your common interests, to learning what they want, to talking about what you do. Once your new friend learns what you do, they become a customer or new client.

This is all made possible because you've initially identified the best people to talk to based on the information they provided about themselves in their Profiles.

The game

First Base   You make a new friend.
Second Base Your new friend learns what you do.
Third Base Your new friend wants what you're selling.
Home Plate Your new friend becomes your customer or client

Getting to first base

The start of any relationship on the Internet begins as soon as someone responds favorably to your initial Instant Message. Only when someone answers your Instant Message are you on first base. There are some important steps to you need to take to get to first base with anyone.

An appealing, creative Screen Name and detailed Profile set the stage for you to be immediately liked by everyone you contact, especially when you have mutual interests, or you appear to be a very interesting person. Every person you talk to has to like you before you can expect them to like what you're promoting.

In baseball, when you step up to the plate, you don't swing at every pitch. You wait for the right pitch, one that you can hit out of the park. Online, you wait for the right person to contact. As you do your search in the Member Directory, you'll find there are millions of people Online while you're searching. You'll be amazed at how many choices you have. You need to be very selective in who you contact or you will waste a lot of time talking to the wrong people.

A search in any Member Directory only takes a few seconds and gives you hundreds of choices. You don't want to swing at the first pitch or contact the first Profile you look at unless it's a good one. Invest your time searching the Member Directory and read through posted Profiles to find someone with an appealing Profile. It doesn't take long when you know what you're looking for.

You will recognize a good Profile when you see it, just like Babe Ruth knew when to swing at a good pitch. When you send an Instant Message to someone with an outstanding Profile and they respond to you, you have made an Internet connection and you're on your way to making a new friend.

Your chance of getting to first base with anyone is directly proportional to the amount of initial interest they have in you.

If the person you're contacting can relate to your Screen Name and/or Profile, they will respond to your Instant Message. People like talking to people that like the same things they do.

People like talking to interesting people

- Do they like your Screen Name and Profile?
- Are they curious about who you are or why you contacted them?
- Do you appear to have things or interests in common?
- Are they willing to interrupt what they are doing to begin an Instant Message conversation with you?

While searching the Member Directory, if you come across an interesting Profile of someone who is not Online, you can add their Screen Name to your Buddy List and save yourself some future searching time.

Create a special "Want to meet" group on your Buddy List and add the Screen Names of the great people that aren't Online when you are. When the person's Screen Name appears on your Buddy List the next time you're Online, it means they are logged into the Instant Messaging system and available to hear from you. You can contact them any time they appear on your Buddy List. After an initial conversation, make sure you move their Screen Name to your regular Buddy List.

If someone you contact doesn't respond, it's most likely that they don't see your Instant Message. Perhaps they're not in front of their computer or they are doing something else Online and have their Instant Messaging system minimized.

Your Screen Name and Profile set the stage for your initial Instant Message conversation to go well. Your initial Instant

Message will be the first thing they see and the message it contains will determine the type of response you get, if you get a response.

Your initial Instant Message should:

- Be complimentary
- Let the person know who you are
- Let the person know what you have in common with them
- Ask an open ended question that the person would want to answer in more than one word

---

First base – you make a new friend.

Once someone has responded to your Instant Message you're on first base and the fun really starts. You're in direct contact with someone that can become your next best friend, new client, or new customer. The person wouldn't have responded if he or she didn't like your Screen Name or Profile, or the content of your initial message. Your relationship will get stronger as you learn more about each other. Instant Message conversations are enjoyable when you're talking to the right person.

Keep in mind that you can't see the person you're typing to, so you really don't know what they are doing while they're answering you. They may welcome your Instant Message as an opportunity to take a break from a boring task. You can count on them to let you know if they are too busy to chat.

If they're involved in a big project, they may only have a few minutes to chat. You can ask *"Did I catch you at a good time?"* If this is the case, you can ask *"When would be a better time to try to reconnect with you later?"*

You can always assume that someone has a little time to chat or they wouldn't have responded to your Instant Message in the first place.

The real art of conversation is not only to say the right thing at the right time, but also to leave unsaid the wrong thing at the tempting moment. Don't be in a hurry and rush to talk about your business. Before a person is going to be interested in your business, the person must be interested in you.

You only have one chance to make a good first impression.

You may have one or several Instant Message conversations with someone before you can really say that person is a new friend. Sometimes having three or four brief five minute Instant Message conversations with someone over a few days or weeks can solidify a relationship faster than one twenty-minute conversation.

Once an Instant Message connection has been made, it's appropriate to add the person's email address to your address book so you can keep the lines of communication going. You may not see someone Online as often as you like. Sending email to your Online friends will keep you in their thoughts.

Your Online relationships with people grow the more contact you have with them. In addition to your Instant Message conversations, you can send email containing jokes, motivational messages, greeting cards, or interesting articles that you think they'll appreciate.
(See Appendix E – Helpful resources)

Every email you send is another reminder about you and keeps you in their thoughts between your Instant Message conversations. You can email your new friend often, as long as the content of your mail is appreciated. Don't send business-related email until you've discussed your business.

Everyone has a story. Who is your new Online friend? What are the missing details between the lines of his or her Profile? Can he or she use your product or service? While learning people's stories, you will discover what they need and want. Until you know what people need and want, you can't help them get it.

You have two ears and one mouth because you're supposed to listen twice as much as you talk

Ask your new friends important pre-qualifying questions as part of your naturally friendly conversation and listen to the answers you receive.

You may decide during your Instant Message conversation that the person you're talking to isn't really a good prospect and doesn't need what you're promoting. Or, they might not be in the market for what you're selling at the moment, but will be at some future time.

Once you're confident that your new Online friend can use what your service or product offers, it's time to let them know what you do.

Second base – your new friend learns what you do

As you share and exchange stories and experiences with your new Online friend, you'll both discover if he or she has an interest or a need for your service or product.

When your new Online friend asks about your business, you're on second base. During the normal course of your Online conversation, the subject of what you do is bound to come up. It's appropriate to talk about your business when your friend asks about it, or you can bring it up yourself after you have determined that your new Online friend needs it or is open to hearing about it.

Sometimes the best way to ask a new friend for business is to ask for the business indirectly. Ask if your new friend knows of anyone who would be interested in doing business with you. This offers your friend an out if they are not interested without making them uncomfortable by saying no to you or your ideas directly.

On the other hand, they may be very interested in your services or products. In this way, you provide an avenue for them to "initiate" the relationship by asking you questions regarding your services or products. This is called a third-party approach. The third-party approach allows you to maintain rapport with your friend without the pressure of rejection.

Just because you're not going to your warm market doesn't mean that the people you talk to Online won't go to theirs. Most people will tell many of their friends what they're doing.

You can find out anything you want to know about people by asking them some simple questions. To ensure that you'll always get the answers you want, use this approach. Start asking questions that give you additional background information about them. Make a statement about yourself and then ask your new friend a question on the same subject in the same Instant Message. This conversational style obligates the other person to respond to you and always guarantees you'll get an answer to your question. For example:

I'm 53. How old are you?

I'm in Orlando, today. Where are you?

I've been Online for two years. How long have you been Online?

I've been playing golf for 11 years. How long have you been playing? I'm a seven handicap golfer. What's your handicap?

I'm a Virgo. What sign are you?

My favorite food is Italian. What's yours?

I've been in real estate for 15 years. How long have you been selling real estate?

I noticed in your Profile that you are a physician. I've been in mutual funds for 15 yrs. How long have you been a doctor?

This form of Online questioning obligates the other person to answer you. This conversational style works in Instant Messages, during telephone conversations, and in face-to-face situations too. The more you learn about someone, the easier it is for you to decide if you want to bring up the subject of your business.

When you ask your Online friends, what they do, they'll usually ask what you do.

One of the reasons you contact people is that, in addition to the fact that you have things in common and would generally like each other if you met, their Profile indicates something that tells you they would make a good client or customer.

Questions to ask yourself

- Could they use your product or service?
- Would they appreciate hearing more details about what you do?
- Are they open to doing business with you?

Paula Pritchard and Kathy Robbins, two of the most successful women in the history of the direct sales industry, created sales organizations of hundreds of thousands of people through their Warm Market referrals. They would ask their friends, "Do you know anyone that is successful, ambitious and dissatisfied with their current situation?" You can ask the same question of every new friend you make Online if you are a recruiter or looking for sales reps for your company.

Just because you're not going to your Warm Market doesn't mean that the people you talk to Online won't go to theirs. Most of the people you contact will tell many of their friends what they're doing.

When the time comes to discuss what you're promoting in an Instant Message, keep it simple. It's always more effective to direct your new friend to a web site, a series of web sites or pre-recorded conference calls than to type long explanations describing your business in an Instant Message.

You can discuss your business using Instant Messaging or wait until you talk to them on the telephone. It's purely a matter of your personal preference. Some people prefer using Instant Messaging to establish a relationship and determine the person's interest or need in a product or service prior to talking about it on the telephone.

When the person you're having an Instant Message conversation with is ready, he or she will be agreeable to move from typing to talking. People will only be open to speaking to you when they like you, trust you, and want to hear more about who you are and what you do.

The more interesting you appear to be, the more interested your new Online friend will be in talking to you. Even if a person genuinely needs what you are promoting, a person has to like you and trust you before he or she will agree to talk to you.

Women, particularly, will not give out their phone numbers to a strange man they meet on the Internet unless they trust them. It's always advisable for women to initially give men a cell phone number to call.

At the appropriate time, you can move from typing to talking on the phone with a simple Instant Message such as:

> *I type with four fingers and two of them need spell check. Would you be up for talking on the phone? It's easier than typing.*

> *There is nothing worse than a slow typist with a lot to say. LOL. Would you be up for talking on the phone? I'd be happy to give you a call or you can call me. What's your preference?*

> *My fingers are starting to ache with all this typing. Would you be up for talking on the phone? I'd be happy to give you a call. When would be a good time to talk?*

Ask your friends qualifying questions

Successful sales people ask qualifying questions during their conversations to determine if the person they're talking to is a serious customer. They also want to know a person's time table for action.

Every type of business has six to eight qualifying questions that can be asked to help a salesperson identify customers. What are the qualifying questions you need to ask someone to determine if he or she is a potential customer for your business?

If you don't know the relevant questions for your business, you need to find out what they are. If you know them, you'll find the people you connect with after doing your searches will answer them during your Instant Message conversation.

There are specific questions used by stockbrokers, insurance salespeople, realtors, car salespeople, yacht brokers, and everyone in business, that are unique to their product or service.

Once you have your qualifying questions ready, you're going to find you have many options and choices on who you're going to talk to.

List the eight qualifying questions for your business:

1. _____

   _____

2. _____

   _____

3. _____

   _____

4. _____

   _____

5. _____

   _____

6. _____

   _____

7. _____

   _____

8. _____

Third base – your new friend wants what you're selling

Successful sales people know that they're not in the convincing business, they're in the sorting business. You don't need or want to push what you're selling on someone. You just want to introduce it to them after you know they can use it or probably want it.

You knew prior to getting to first base with someone that they most likely could use what you're promoting because you read their Profile. Once you made contact, you learned even more about them to know that they need and want your product or service. You knew as you were talking to them on second base that you could help them. Third base is the place and time to let them sell themselves on you and what you do.

Your Online relationship deepens with every contact you have with someone. Following up with people and staying in touch with them is as important to your success as making the initial contact.

Sales statistics

48% of sales people never follow up with a prospect

25% of sales people make a second contact and stop

12% of sales people only make three contacts and stop

Only 10 % of sales people make more than three contacts

2% of sales are made on the first contact

3% of sales are made on the second contact

5% of sales are made on the third contact

10% of sales are made on the fourth contact

80% of sales are made on the fifth to twelfth contact

Don't be in a rush to push your business or products on your new Online friends. Remember 80 percent of sales are made on the fifth to twelfth contact.

Home run

When your new Online friend realizes that they need what you're promoting and they become your customer or client, you've hit a home run. When your new friend asks for your help or your offer to help them is graciously accepted, you've hit a home run.

But scoring a home run and winning the game are two different things. Your relationship with your new friend has only just begun when you do some business. A good, mutually-beneficial relationship can last a long time. Or, it can fizzle and fade if it's not continuously attended to. Time will tell.

CHAPTER 11

How to start a conversation and make a new friend

The real art of conversation is not only to say the right thing at the right time, but also to leave unsaid the wrong thing at the tempting moment.

Just like in the real face-to-face world, you only have one opportunity to make a good first impression with someone. One of the nice things about meeting people Online is that you can Instant Message people while you're wearing your pajamas. And, you don't have to worry about your make-up or if you're having a bad hair day.

The Screen Name and Profile you've created provides the person you're contacting with an idea of who you are, but it's going to be your opening Instant Message line to someone that will start the conversational ball rolling. The key is to find something in a person's Profile to comment on. The words people put in their Profile are their open invitation for you to contact them.

The following Instant Message opening lines or a variation of them will melt the ice with a stranger and start you on the way to meeting and making some wonderful new friends. Since you've pre-selected who you're contacting by reviewing their Screen Name and Profile, each one of these new friends should also be an ideal prospect for your business, when it's time to talk about your business. Don't rush to talk about your business until it's appropriate.

Your initial Instant Message can focus on any section of a Profile. You can make reference to their Screen Name, location, marital status, gender, hobby, occupation, personal quote or anything they list in their posted Profile.

Screen Name openings

Good Morning, I was searching the directory and noticed your Screen Name. I'm intrigued, how did you come up with your Screen Name? What's the story? Did I catch you at a good time?

Hello, you have an interesting Screen Name and Profile. I hope I'm not interrupting

Hi, my name is (your name), You've created a real interesting and catchy Screen Name. Is there a story behind it you can share? Do you have a few minutes to talk?

Hello, I was looking to see who was Online and noticed your Profile. What's the significance of the numbers in your Screen Name? :-)

Hi, I love your Screen Name. I wish I had thought of it. Is there a story behind it? Hope I'm not interrupting.

Location openings

Hello, I notice your Profile says you're in Pensacola. How did you fare during the hurricanes last month?

Hi there. My name is (your name). I just moved to Tampa in the summer. Have you lived here very long?

Hello, My name is (your name) I'm coming to San Diego for my vacation next month. What's the weather like during this time of the year?

Hello, I was taking a break and did a random search in the Membership Directory and noticed your Profile. It's really a good one. How is the weather in Chicago?   :-)

Hi, I just did a random search to see who was Online here in <u>Chicago</u> (Insert the appropriate city) and you have the best Profile next to mine LOL.   How long have you been in <u>sales and marketing</u>? (Insert the appropriate career) (LOL = Internet jargon for laugh out loud)

Marital status openings

Hello, My name is (your name) I've been married for 29 years. How long have you been married?

Hello, My name is (your name) I like your Profile. I've been married for ten years and have three kids ages - 5,7,9. I see you've got three kids too. How old are yours?

Hobby or interest openings

Hello, My name is (your name). I like what you did with your Profile. I've been sailing for over 40 years. What kind of boat do you sail?

Hello, I noticed your Profile while doing a search for people that liked to play tennis. I've been playing tennis for 12 years. How long have you been playing tennis?

Occupation openings

Hello, I like what you did with your Profile. How long have you been a <u>personal trainer</u>? (Insert the appropriate career).

Hello, I see I'm not the only insomniac up this early. I like your Profile. What got you up so early today?

Hello, I noticed in your Profile you quote Socrates. That's my favorite quote too. I manage a large office with 22 people. What kind of business do you manage? :-)

Hi, I'm snowed in along with everyone else in town and turned to the directory to find intelligent life. I'm in retail sales, what do you do?

Hello, my name is (your name). I've been in insurance sales for 12 yrs. How long have you been in sales? :-)

Hello, my name is (your name). I've been sailing since I was 12 and have a 39' sailboat. Where do you do your sailing? :-)

Hello, Do you believe all the (snow, rain, wind, etc.) we're having today? How long have you been a (doctor, lawyer, chiropractor, manager, sales rep, etc.)?

Hello, I can't watch another minute of this bad football game so I went Online to find someone interesting to talk to. You've got a sharp Profile. Do you have a few minutes to talk to someone that's sharp too. LOL

Hello, I see I'm not the only insomniac up this late. I like your Profile. What's keeping you up so late tonight?

Hello, I see I'm not the only insomniac up at this hour. I notice your Profile says you're in sales. What do you sell? :-)

Your opening line should be friendly and complimentary. As in any form of initial contact (face-to-face, phone, Instant Message), it's appropriate to introduce yourself. Providing your first name is all that is necessary.

You never know what someone is doing when you send them an Instant Message. Their answer will tell you if they have time to talk to you. Instant Messaging and proper telephone etiquette are similar.

When you call someone on the telephone, the first thing you should say after "Hello" is:

- **"Is this a good time to talk?" or**
- **"Do you have a few minutes to talk?" or**
- **"Did I catch you at a good time?"**

This same courtesy is appreciated Online when you send someone an Instant Message. It gives the person on the other end the chance to tell you if it's convenient to talk.

If people don't have time to talk at the moment, you can put them on your Buddy List and contact them later. The important thing is that you've made contact and they have responded. They may even reply by telling you when it would be more convenient for them to talk. If this happens, you know the next time you contact them they will be very receptive to talking to you.

Hello!! :-)

Sometimes, just typing "hello" with a smiling face icon will begin an Instant Message conversation with someone. You must have a fabulous Screen Name and a Profile that really grabs someone's attention, and they must have a great deal in common with you for this one word Instant Message to start a conversation.

Keep in mind that before people answer your Instant Message, they're going to check out your Profile to see who you are and what you're all about. They're wondering what your Online agenda is. Why are you contacting them? They'll check your Profile to see if you're selling something. If your Profile is an advertisement for your business, they will delete your Instant Message as fast as you delete the junk email you receive.

If someone likes your Screen Name and Profile they'll respond. If they don't have time to talk to you at the moment, they'll tell you nicely and ask you to talk later. The more interesting you appear to someone, the more likely it is that they will want to talk to you.

If your Instant Message focuses on a person's Screen Name or Profile, your chances of receiving a response are pretty high. Listed below are variations of good ice-breaking Instant Messages:

Paying someone a compliment in an Instant Message is always an effective Online ice breaker. Adding a smiling face to the end of your comment is a sign of friendship and tells the other person you're smiling. Giving someone Online the impression you're smiling is as easy as typing a colon : then a dash – then the back end of a parenthesis) Put them all together and you've got a smiling face :-)

Hello, it's great to see someone with a nice Profile. It's nice to see so many interesting, intelligent people on AOL (Yahoo, ICQ, MSN, etc.) I've been Online for three years – how long have you been Online?

People who have taken the time to create a nice Profile and publish details about themselves in the Member Directory are open to talking to you. That's why they created their Profile in the first place. Making a flattering remark about someone's Profile is a very effective way to initiate a conversation. It also says that you think he or she is intelligent at the same time. This opening line is hard for a person to resist responding to.

> *Hello, am I interrupting? I'm a 55-year-old dentist. How long have you been a dentist?*

When you offer information about yourself in your opening Instant Message and ask a question at the same time, the other person feels obligated to answer your question. Everything people have posted in their Profile is open to discussion. Since they indicated what their occupation is in their Profile, talking about their work is appropriate. People love to talk about themselves. You'll learn a lot about them by asking questions about what they do.

> *Hello, I was taking a break from a perfectly fabulous day to surf the membership directory and noticed your Profile. Do you have a few minutes to talk? This is a terrific way to meet new people.*

This opening line tells someone you're a positive person with the use of the words perfectly, fabulous and terrific. People's answers will tell you if they have time to talk. If they don't, you're going to want to find out when it would be more convenient for them to talk.

> *Hello, I notice that you're a doctor. I work with other doctors. What kind of a doctor are you?*

> *Hello, I notice that you're a doctor. I work with other doctors. How long have you been practicing medicine?*

You're going to be amazed at how easy it is to talk to a doctor or any other busy professional Online. In fact, you have easier access to talking to a doctor Online then you do if you tried to see him at his office.

In most cases you just can't pick up the phone and call a doctor. You have to get past his gatekeepers – office manager, staff. Part of their job is to insulate him and screen his calls.

Yet, doctors are Online during their breaks to check stock prices, to make travel plans, to do research, or to do other things. Your Instant Message is just the opportunity for a physician to kick back and take a break. If you've got an interesting Screen Name and Profile, and your opening Instant Message is appealing, you'll get a response from a doctor.

> *Hello, I have been a stockbroker for several years. I really enjoy it. What do you most enjoy about being a stockbroker?*

This is a very effective way to begin an Online conversation with someone that works in your field. It's a good Online ice breaker.

Pay close attention to the answers you get from the people you're talking to. Remember what kind of people you're looking for. You're looking for people who give positive, encouraging answers.

At any time if you're not happy with someone's answers, you should politely end the conversation and start a new one with someone else. To politely end a conversation, type,

I'm sorry I have to go. Have a nice day.
Bye for now.

Just be yourself when it comes to talking to people Online. The conversational approaches that work for you in any face-to-face situation will work Online too. If you've already got your approach down when you contact people in the real world, don't be afraid to try it Online. It will work there too.

Michael was never at a loss to meet people. He became successful without the Internet and initially couldn't be bothered with it. Then he heard that one of his co-workers had landed the biggest account in the history of his company from the Internet. That piece of news inspired him to create the following Profile.

TravelingMichael1

Member Name:	**Michael**
Location:	**Boca Raton, FL**
Sex:	**Male**
Marital Status:	**Happily Married w/ 2 great kids**
Hobbies:	**International Travel, Sailing, Fine Dining Baseball, Aerobic Floating, Making New Friends**
Favorite Gadgets:	**Laptop, cell phone, remote control - not necessarily in that order!**
Occupation:	**Extraordinary Sales Executive earning my PhD in travel**
Personal Quote:	**Success is not to be pursued; it is to be attracted by the person we become.**

Michael's company sold supplies to chiropractors. After creating his Profile, he searched the Member Directory looking for some local chiropractors to contact and found Dr Makewell.

DRMAKEWELL98

Member Name:	**Brian**
Location:	**Boca Raton, FL USA**
Sex:	**Male**
Marital Status:	**Yes**
Hobbies:	**Family, Hockey, Harley**
Favorite Gadgets:	**My hands**
Occupation:	**Chiropractor**
Personal Quote:	**Check out www.fixpinchednerves.com**

TravelingMichael1: **I was taking a break and came across your Profile. I love your web site. How did you get such a great URL?**

DRMAKEWELL98: **actually, i was sitting around 1 night and came up with a bunch of them**

TravelingMichael1: **I bet there are a lot of Docs that wish they jumped on that one! Good job!**

DRMAKEWELL98: **did you look at the site?**

TravelingMichael1: **Yes I did, Great site. Did you do it?**

DRMAKEWELL98: **i have a guy who does the tech stuff are you a chiropractor?**

TravelingMichael1: **No but I work with a number of them.**

DRMAKEWELL98: **where?**

TravelingMichael1: **all over but I live in Boca**

DRMAKEWELL98: **me too, but maybe you knew that
who do you work with???
what exactly do you do for them?**

TravelingMichael1: **I work with them to overcome some of
the pain that managed care has caused**

DRMAKEWELL98: **tell me about it.
it stinks**

TravelingMichael1: **that's for sure
you guys work hard enough**

DRMAKEWELL98: **why don't you give me a call... ###-####**

TravelingMichael1: **ok**

Michael moved from first base to second base in this short Instant Message series. Michael called Brian and they spoke on the telephone for over an hour. Brian was interested in the products Michael's company provided and agreed to meet him the following day to discuss them further. Within twenty-four hours, Michael moved around all the bases and scored a home run. Brian's order was big enough to help Michael win his company's monthly sales contest. Brian subsequently referred a friend to Michael who placed the biggest order for products in the history of the company that eclipsed the previous record by twenty percent.

A direct no-nonsense approach

For the people in sales that aren't into creating relationships with their clients or customers, Instant Messaging can still help you find new clients and customers.

There is no attempt to establish a relationship in the Instant Message example below. Your Online prospect must have a detailed Profile which is their invitation for you to contact them.

The person you contact must answer each of your Instant Message statements in an affirmative and positive manner or it's not a good idea to send them any information on your company. If you do, it will be considered unsolicited business email – SPAM.

If they give you permission to send them email on your company, then it's obviously not unsolicited. You'll probably receive a few "no's," but you'll fill up a pipeline of interested prospects with the ones that say "yes." You won't have a relationship with these people until you take the time to develop one.

First Instant Message after you find a suitable Profile that is filled with information

Hello... You are probably wondering why I am saying Hello specifically to you out of over 25 million members of AOL... LOL. I hope I'm not interrupting.

(Wait for their reply, when you get a positive response, copy and paste the following)

> *I was scanning member Profiles and yours caught my eye. Time is our most precious asset and I truly respect yours. From one professional to another professional, do I have your permission to be direct?*

You must wait for their reply. Since you haven't taken any time to make the person like you, their natural walls of resistance against sales people will be up.

> *I represent a very dynamic company that is changing the lives of many people in North America. Your Profile says that you're a (CPA) in (St. Louis). It happens that (St. Louis) has been targeted as a high-growth area for our company. Would you be interested in learning more about my company and the opportunity it may present to you? It's been of interest to many other (CPAs). If you are not interested, perhaps you know someone that may be?*

(Wait for their reply)

> *With your permission I would like to email you some information about how people are capitalizing on this inevitable trend. Is that OK with you?*

(Wait for their reply)

> *Thank you for your time and a have a safe and prosperous day.*

(Wait for their reply)

> *Your information will be arriving shortly. If you feel it's something you're interested in, I'd love to talk to you about it. If not, perhaps you know someone that is looking for an opportunity. Again, Thanks for your time.*

You need a good Screen Name and Profile to make any Instant Message strategy work. If people don't like your Screen Name and Profile, they're not going to like you, and will not respond.

Elliott was a successful entrepreneur that created the Screen Name LAREBROKER, and posted the following Profile for others to see:

LAREBROKER

Member Name:	**Elliot**
Location:	**Beverly Hills, CA**
Sex:	**Male**
Marital Status:	**More times than Liz Taylor**
Hobbies:	**Real Estate, Investment Banking, V.P. Residential & Commercial Mortgages**
Computers:	**Use them All**
Occupation:	**CEO Internet Startup, Computer Consultant - Real Estate Broker**
Personal Quote:	**If you can't dazzle someone with brilliance, then baffle them with BS**

Elliott was having a hard time finding someone to run his Internet startup. He searched the Member Directory for people who listed "CEO" in their Profiles. He considered the Online Profiles an abbreviated version of a person's resume.

He found someone with an interesting Profile and initiated a conversation by typing:

LAREBROKER:
> Hi, I just read your Profile. You're a very interesting man.

TheLeadDog:
> Thanks. You've got an interesting Profile and humorous personal quote.

LAREBROKER:
> I just got an Internet patent and I'm looking for a CEO.

TheLeadDog:
> What do you expect your CEO to do?

LAREBROKER:
> I'm looking for someone to run an Internet company for me. It's got an Online match making theme using email addresses on bumper stickers

TheLeadDog:
> Perhaps we should talk. I know a few people.

LAREBROKER:
> mmmmmmmm OK, I thought you might

TheLeadDog:
> How did you happen to find me?

LAREBROKER:
> Profile in Member Directory

TheLeadDog:
> Give me a call.......XXX-XXX-XXXX

LAREBROKER:
> Can you call me?

TheLeadDog:
> Sure, I can call you in ten minutes. What's your number?

CHAPTER 12

Why Instant Messaging beats Chat Rooms

Before Instant Messaging became as popular as it is today, Chat Rooms were the place where people would engage in a virtual dialog with other people who shared their interest in a particular subject.

Instant Messaging popularity has turned each Instant Messaging system into one big Chat Room.

You can talk to a stranger directly and privately with an Instant Message, a luxury not available when you're talking in a Chat Room. Most of the people that use Instant Messaging would never take the time to visit a Chat Room.

You can go through a list of Chat Rooms and find one called "Nurses Online" with thirty people in it. However, not all of the people there would be nurses and not everyone would have a personal Profile. There would be people in the Chat Room that wanted to talk to nurses as well as nurses themselves. But you'd only have access to those thirty people.

Or, you can search the Member Directory of any Instant Messaging system and find thousands of nurses on a worldwide basis that have personal Profiles. All of them are Online and available to receive your Instant Message. You can contact any one of them. The amount of information people list in their Profile is directly proportional to their willingness to receive an Instant Message from a stranger.

Talking to people in Chat Rooms in most cases is a waste of your time when you consider how easy it is to send someone an Instant Message.

Yet Chat Rooms are very popular. The number of Chat Rooms on the Internet is clear evidence of their popularity.

The rational of Chat Room defenders over Instant Messaging usage is that the people you find in Chat Rooms are there to meet and chat with others. They feel that sending an Instant Message to someone you don't know is intrusive, After all, just because someone is Online doesn't mean that they are agreeable to having an Instant Message conversation. What these people miss is that you're not trying to talk to everyone that uses Yahoo's Instant Messenger. You're contacting only those people who have taken the time and trouble to fill out a complete Profile. Their Profile is your open invitation to contact them.

A Chat Room is nothing more than another window on your computer screen that gives you direct access to a number of other people that have logged into the same room. Most Chat Rooms support 20 to 30 people. Once a Chat Room is full, no one else can gain entry until someone leaves.

As this book was written to be the complete guide to networking through Instant Messaging, the rest of this chapter provides details on ways people use Instant Messaging and Chat Rooms effectively.

The direct links to some of the popular Chat Rooms on the Internet are found below. I list them because this book covers all phases of Instant Messaging. You can send an Instant Message to someone in a Chat Room and have a private conversation with them out of the view of the other people in the room (Lofting). While you can meet other people in a Chat Room, it's not the most efficient use of your time.

Chat Rooms can be found at

AOL	http://www.aol.com/community/chat/allchats.html
ICQ	http://www.icq.com/icqchat
Yahoo	http://chat.yahoo.com
Talk City	http://www.talkcity.com
MSN Chat	http://chat.msn.com/

I've studied the Chat Room phenomenon first hand. It amazes me. There are Chat Rooms on every imaginable subject, and some discussing subjects that I could never imagine in my wildest dreams.

There are Chat Rooms that people frequent at certain times of the day to connect with their Internet friends and to make new friends. At certain times of the day you can't get into some Chat Rooms, even if you want to.

The problem with Chat Rooms

Chat Rooms limit the number of people that can be in the room at one time. You have greater access to more people and better choices by searching the Member Directory for people that are Online when you are.

Many of the people found in Chat Rooms don't have Profiles telling you about them. Many people create a Screen Name just to enter the room and delete the name once they're done talking to others. To save time, you want to talk to someone with a good Profile that has something in common with you. You are not interested in chatting with everyone in the room.

It's hard to have a nice conversation in a Chat Room with one person. Everyone else there can read what you're typing and can interject and interrupt the flow of your conversation.

Chat Rooms have developed a bad reputation. It seems like every story you hear in the news about people having a bad experience with someone they met on the Internet started in a Chat Room.

People that spend time in Chat Rooms get more junk email peddling adult web sites than people who never visit one. Online peddlers of adult web sites routinely harvest (collect) the Screen Names of everyone in a Chat Room at a particular time of day. Once these Internet outlaws have your Screen Name they have the email address connected to the Instant Messaging system you're using. Then the SPAM begins. The email you receive from them will be directed toward getting you to visit one of their adult web sites.

Everyone gets junk mail today. Perhaps it's only a trickle, but you can expect the trickle to turn into a stream of SPAM once you visit a Chat Room. If you make the mistake of clicking on a link that takes you an adult website, the stream turns into a river.

Chat Room Tips

The name of a Chat Room tells you the topic being discussed. The words used in the Screen Names and Profiles of the people in the room will tell you if you want to be there.

Read the Profile of everyone in a Chat Room before you talk to them. The words in their Screen Name and Profile indicate their Online agenda and what they like to talk about.

If you find someone with an appealing Screen Name and Profile and you want to talk to them directly, you can send them an Instant Message and chat privately, out of the view of everyone else in the room. You'll find that everyone is more open and candid when they're talking to you in a private Instant Message than when twenty two other people are reading their words.

Don't talk to someone without a Profiles unless they're willing to tell you all about themselves in the early part of your conversation. If someone without a Profile attempts to talk to you in a Chat Room or through an Instant Message, it's an acceptable practice to ask them questions about who they are prior to talking about anything else.

WingedCrusader: **hey diva!! what part of south beach do you live in?**

ThePoolsideDiva: **why don't you have a Profile... no Profile, no chat**

WingedCrusader: **i'm new – haven't made it yet**

ThePoolsideDiva: **tell me about yourself – my Profile tells you all about me**

WingedCrusader: **what do you want to know?**

ThePoolsideDiva: **you can start with your name, age, where you live, your gender, list your hobbies, and tell me what you do**

WingedCrusader: **anything else?**

ThePoolsideDiva: **oh sure...your social security and American Express numbers LOL**

WingedCrusader: **my name is Mitchell, I'm 12**

Remember, you only have so much time to spend Online talking to someone. You want your time to be well spent. The time you spend talking to someone that **might** be interesting could be spent talking to someone that you **know** is interesting.

Two ways creating your own Chat Room can be more effective than going into an existing one.

1. **You can create a Chat Room to introduce your business to one of your existing Online friends**

2. **You can create a Chat Room to attract someone that is interested or curious about the Chat Room name or topic being discussed**

Use a Chat Room to introduce your business to one of your existing Online friends

From: Laurie
To: YourOnlineMentor

Hello Max;

I thoroughly enjoyed listening to the Internet Training call on Monday night. I have enjoyed working with you and have put many of your ideas to work that you have shared with me. I did something a bit different the other day when I set up my Chat Room that worked very well and I thought you could use it to help others as well...it is my gift back to you.
First I set up my Chat Room for the business I am promoting. I did this with a friend of mine I'm working with. We both were in the room alone. I was a little nervous and wondered if any prospects would come in.
It was boring waiting for people to find me so I looked at my Buddy List and noticed one of my buddies was Online. I sent her an Instant Message and asked her to please come in my Chat Room and let me practice on her. I told her that I

had set up a room for my business and needed to practice answering questions and improve my typing skills.
I told her to ask me anything and when we were finished to please tell me how I did. Was I too pushy? Did I answer all her questions clearly? etc. You see she and I have been buddies for a few months and I respected her opinion.
As we went through the practice session, she got so excited about the product that she ordered it. Max, I did this again with another buddy a few days later and the same thing happened. This time my buddy lived here in Albuquerque so he came over and bought some – he loves it too! I went into a Chat Room the other day and he was promoting the product there too. I was very impressed with the results and Max, no one felt pressured. Best of all, I didn't insult a friend by pushing my business.
Max I want to thank you again for all your support and help...Please share this information freely.

Sincerely, Laurie.

You can create a Chat Room to attract someone that is interested or curious about the Chat Room name or the topic being discussed

Creating a Chat Room with an interesting topic name will attract people just like a good Screen Name and Profile. You can use any of the names in Appendix B and add Online as a Prefix or Suffix. Example: Doctors Online or Online Doctors. Accountants Online, Golfers Online, Sailors Online, Nurses Online, Teachers Online, Happy In Indiana, Millionaires Lounge, Successful Women, etc.

Multi-task in a Chat Room

You can create a Chat Room and then search the Member Directory looking for people to talk to instead of waiting for people to come into the room.

You can create a Chat Room and go shopping. Once the room is set up, you don't have to sit in front of your computer. Go Shopping!! You can check later to see who entered your room while you were gone. You can learn a great deal about anyone that tries to talk to you while you are away by reading their Profile and their attempt to get you to respond to them.

NurseBetty:

> **Hi, why are you in the room all by yourself?**
> **are you there?**
> **I'm sorry I missed you....you must be busy**
> **I liked your Profile. If you see me Online say hello**

OR

AnnTheNurse:

> **Hi, why are you in the room all by yourself?**
> **are you there?**
> **why won't you talk to me?**
> **it's RUDE not to respond to me**
> **who do you think you are?**
> **You are RUDE**
> **I've got better things to do than trying to talk to you**
> **take a long walk off a short pier...**
> **you jerk**

Who would you contact when you return from shopping? NurseBetty or AnnTheNurse?

You can send the following email to NurseBetty if she's no longer Online. Betty should recognize your Screen Name from being in the Chat Room and your mail will get through.

From: Jacyln294
To: NurseBetty

Hi Betty, I'm sorry I missed you in the chat room. I like your profile. I've added you to my buddy list. Please feel free to add me to yours. The next time you're online say hello. I'll do the same. I look forward to connecting with you. Bye for now

Jacyln

CHAPTER 13

Internet etiquette and safety

You only have one time to make a good impression with anyone so it's important to know about Internet etiquette. I've included a few common dos and don'ts to help you.

The Internet gives you access to some wonderful people, but it also has a dark side. If you think there is good in everybody, you haven't met everybody. And you don't want to.

In most cases you're going to be able to identify the people you want to avoid by reading their Screen Name and Profile.

You need to take some simple steps to protect yourself and your computer to enjoy the Internet and all the good things the world wide web has to offer.

The things you WANT to do

Keep your computer safe from emailed viruses with a reliable anti-virus software package like Norton or McAfee.

Always send an initial Instant Message that makes complimentary remarks about something in someone's Profile that would make them smile. Be complimentary. Refer to what they've posted in their personal Profile.

Always review the Profile of anyone sending you an Instant Message. If you don't like the contents of the message or anything in the Profile of the sender, delete it.

Always send original email. If you receive something in an email that you want to share with someone, take the time to copy and paste the contents of the old email into a new email and send it.

Be yourself.

Be polite and courteous.

Be organized and keep records of who you're talking to.

Have a good time. The entire process is fun when you're talking to the right people.

The things you NEVER want to do

DO NOT send an Instant Message to a stranger that is a blatant sales pitch. (SPIM)

 Hello, If I could show you a way to make a few hundred dollars a month working part time from home on the Internet, would you be interested?

 I'm looking for a few people interested in making some serious money; if you're interested, click here.

 Click here if you'd like to be rich.

DO NOT send an email that promotes your company, product or service to someone you don't know. (SPAM)

DO NOT take the e-mail addresses in an e-mail you receive from someone else and send promotional material to that list of people. If you do, you're SPAMMING.

Do not forward email you've received by clicking on the 'Forward' button. The most annoying thing about receiving forwarded email from someone is that you have to scroll down for extended periods of time until you get to the message. Most people usually get tired of scrolling and close your email without ever seeing what you've sent.

DO NOT send someone you don't know an Instant Message unless you have read their Profile and you can say, "I really like your Profile!!"

DO NOT send someone on your Buddy List an Instant Message as soon as they appear online. Wait until they've been online for at least five minutes. Some Instant Messaging systems are activated as soon as a person goes online. Many people go the Internet several times a day to read their email, to check their bank balance or to look something up. It can be annoying if you contact someone repeatedly the moment they go online.

DO NOT open an attachment in an email from someone you don't know. It could contain a virus.

DO NOT open an attachment in an email from someone you know unless you know what the attachment is. It could contain a virus.

DO NOT send an Instant Message using all capitalized words. This is considered 'shouting' or 'yelling.' For instance, HELLO vs. Hello.

DO NOT click on a link to a web site in an Instant Message from someone you don't know.

DO NOT answer an Instant Message with objectionable content.

You will meet people on the Internet just like you

A man driving with his family to relocate to a new town stopped at a gas station fifty miles from his destination. He asked the attendant, "What kind of people live in the town up ahead? I'm moving there with my family after twenty years living in a city I'd prefer not to mention."

The attendant responded, "What kind of people lived in the town you just came from?"

The man answered, "They were awful people. Dishonest, not to be trusted and very unfriendly! I was miserable the entire time we lived there. I'm glad we left."

The attendant shook his head and replied, "I'm sorry to tell you that the people in the town up ahead are just like the people in your home town. I don't think you're going to be very happy there."

Thirty minutes later another car pulled into the same gas station. The man driving approached the attendant and said, "Excuse me. Could you please give me some information? I'm in the process of moving to the town up ahead. I was wondering if you could tell me, what kind of people live there?"

The attendant said, "What kind of people lived in the town you just came from?"

The man answered, "They were wonderful people. Everyone was friendly, always courteous and helpful. I never had to lock my door. Everyone was honest. People would give you the shirt off their backs. I'm going to miss all my friends."

The attendant smiled, "I'm happy to tell you that the people in the town up ahead are just like the people in your home town. I'm sure you're going to love it there and will make many new friends."

You can find precisely who you want to meet on the Internet now that you know where to find the best people and how to use Instant Messaging. Now that you've finished reading this book you are ready to enjoy the best the Internet has to offer.

Appendices

Make the Internet Your Warm Market

Appendix A

Instant Messaging systems and Search Engines

Yahoo

Found at www.yahoo.com. Yahoo's free Instant Messaging system is used by over 237 million* people making it the biggest IM system on the Internet. The popularity of Yahoo's Search Engine, email services, Chat Rooms and other features propelled them past ICQ in numbers of Internet users. The Yahoo Member Directory can be found at http://members.yahoo.com

In addition to typed text messages, you can also use Yahoo's Instant Messages to exchange voice, video, files, and more with your Online friends.

ICQ

Found at www.ICQ.com. ICQ was the first universal free Instant Messaging system made available to the public in 1996.

ICQ's immediate popularity and amazing growth in their number of users motivated AOL to purchase them in 1998. ICQ was the largest IM system for years until Yahoo became number one. ICQ is used by over 190 million* people. Seventy percent of ICQ users reside outside of the US, in over 243 countries. It is available in 18 languages. ICQ claims its users are connected to ICQ over five hours each day on average.

The ICQ Member Directory where you can identify ICQ users to Instant Message can be found at:
www.icq.com/whitepages

---

* at time of printing

MSN

Found at www.msn.com. MSN's (Microsoft Network) Instant Messaging system is used by over 180 million* users primarily because it comes pre-installed on most new computers. MSN's Member Directory can be found at http://members.msn.com.

You will want to do an "advanced search" in their Member Directory to find the best people to talk to.

AOL

Found at www.aol.com AOL (America Online) is one of the largest ISPs (Internet Service Providers) in the world.

AOL has two Instant Messaging systems. AIM is their free software that can be downloaded off their website and used from anywhere in the world. AIM claims to have over 53 million* users on a worldwide basis. AIM does not give you access to the AOL Member Directory. It permits you to contact the people you place on your Buddy List and offers limited searching ability to find new people.

AOL also has an Instant Messaging system that is part of their subscription-based service. There are a number of subscription price plans, which all require you to install AOL's proprietary software. After you install the software, you have access to an Instant Messaging system, the Member Directory, and many other AOL features. AOL currently claims to have 25 million* users in the United States and another 13 million users in 14 countries.

To access AOL's Member Directory you must be logged in to their subscription based service of AOL. Once logged into AOL - click on Keyword at the top of your computer and type 'Member Directory' or hit the control key on your keyboard and the letter K (Contol + K) then type 'Member Directory.'

AOL's subscription service also provides its members with a free home page where people provide information about themselves. To search the personal web pages of AOL members, go to http://hometown.aol.com

AOL is a good place to start for the Internet 'Newbie.' They have excellent customer service representatives that can be contacted 24 hours a day to help solve any Internet issues.

Other Internet locations using Instant Messaging

Monster.com

Found at www.monster.com. Monster.com, where 40 million* people that are looking for a job pay a monthly fee to make their work resumes visible to everyone, also offers an Instant Messaging feature for a minimal fee.

Online dating sites

Instant Message usage has become so popular that many Online dating sites offer it as an extra feature of their service. Over 40 million* people visit an Online dating site every month. The largest Online dating site is www.match.com. A word search on any of the popular Search Engines listed next will give you an updated list of dating sites.

Class reunion web sites

Class reunion sites enable you to find and connect with old friends from elementary school, high school, college or with people you shared military service with.

www.reunion.com
www.classmates.com

A word search on any of the popular Search Engines listed next will give you an updated list of other class reunion web sites Each of the Instant Messaging systems mentioned offers unique features. It's highly advisable that you check out these free Instant Messaging systems before you make any heavy investments in advertising for prospects or in lead generation campaigns. Finding the best people on the Internet to talk to about your business is as easy as picking a cashew out of a bowl of mixed nuts.

Systems that make Instant Messaging easier

Powertools	www.bpssoft.com
IM Tools	www.imtools.com
Sub Profile	www.subProfile.com
Trillian	www.bigblueball.com

Found at www.bigblueball.com. Trillian is an application that consolidates, in a single interface, IM contacts from a variety of IM services, such as America Online's AIM, Yahoo's Yahoo Messenger, and Microsoft's MSN Messenger. Because most IM services don't interoperate with each other, it's necessary to log on separately to each IM network to communicate with its members. While Trillian doesn't solve the interoperability problem, it does prevent users from having to keep an IM Buddy List interface open for each network.

---

* at time of printing

Internet Search Engines to find other Instant Messaging systems

The following list of popular Search Engines will help you find more information about any subject. As new Instant Messaging communities form on the Internet, you can use any of these Search Engines to find them.

Alta Vista	www.altavista.com
America Online	www.aol.com
Ask Jeeves	www.ask.com
Excite	www.excite.com
Google	www.google.com
HotBot	www.hotbot.com
Lycos	www.lycos.com
Yahoo	www.yahoo.com

Appendix B

Name jogger for Warm Market and Internet searches

Use this list to make your Warm Market list and to do key word searches in any Member Directory. You're looking for people who engage in the activity, the occupation or are interested in the subject.

Accountant	Bicycles	Clubs
Actor	Billiards	Coach
Advertising	Boats	Coins
Aerobics	Book Stores	Collections
Aircraft	Bookkeeping	College
Airline	Books	Computer
Anthony Robbins	Bowling	Construction
Antiques	Boy Scouts	Consultant
Apartment	Boys/Girls Clubs	Contractors
Architect	Broadcasting	Copiers
Art	Broker	Cosmetics
Artist	Builder	Courier
Athlete	Buses	CPA
Attorney	Butcher	Crafts
Auctioneer	Camera	Credit Union
Auditor	Camping	Cruise
Auto Insurance	Cantor	Dairy
Automobile	Car	Day Care
Bakery	Caretaker	Daycare
Band/Orchestra	Carpet Cleaning	Deliveries
Bank	Cattle	Dentist
Banquets	Cellular Phones	Department Store
Barber	Cement	Dermatologist
Bars	Chess	Designer
Baseball	Chiropractor	Detective
Basketball	Christ	Diaper Service
Beach	Church	Diet
Beauty Salon	Civil Engineering	Direct Mail
Beepers	Cleaners	Disk Jockey
Bible	Clothes	Doctor

Driving Range
Drug Store
Dry Clean
eBay
Education
Electrician
Emergency Services
EMS
Engineer
Engineering
Entertainment
Exterminator
Eye Care
Farmer
Farming
Fast Food
Father
Fax Equipment
Film Industry
Fireman
Fisherman
Fishing
Florist
Food Distribution
Food Service
Food Store
Fund Raising
Furniture
Garden
Gift Shop
Girl Scout
Golf
Golfing
Government
Grandfather
Grandma
Grandmother
Grandpa
Graphic Arts
Grocery
Gun

Gymnastics
Hair Stylist
Hand Crafts
Handyman
Hardware
Health Club
Health Insurance
Helicopter
Hiking
Home Improvement
Home Repair
Horse
Hospital
Hotel
HR
Human Resources
Hunting
Ice Skating
Importing
Income Tax
Insurance
Interior Decorating
Interior Decorator
Jaycees
Jesus
Jewelry
Jim Rohn
Judo
Karate
Kindergarten
Kiwanis
Labor Union
Laundry
Law Enforcement
Lawyer
Leasing
Library
Life Insurance
Lighting
Limousine
Lincoln

Lions
Luggage
Mail
Mail Order
Management
Manager
Manufacture
Manufacturing
Mathematician
Mathematics
Mechanic
Men's Clothing
Military
Military Personnel
Mobile Home
Model
Modeling
Mortgage
Mortician
Mosque
Motel
Mother
Music
Napoleon Hill
Night school
Nursery-Plants
Nursing Home
Office Furniture
Office Supplies
Optimist
Optometrist
Pastor
Personal Trainer
Pharmaceutical
Pharmacist
Pharmacy
Phone
Photography
Physician
Plato
Podiatrist

Police	Sheriff	Travel Agency
Preacher	Shoe Store	Travel Agent
Printing	Singer	TV
Psalm 23	Social Services	Upholstery Shop
Psychologist	Socrates	Vacuum Cleaner
Publisher	Sporting Goods	Vendor
Rabbi	Stationery	Veterinarian
Radio	Surveyor	Video
Real Estate	Synagogue	Volunteer
Restaurant	Teacher	Weight Loss
Retail Outlet	Television	Weight Watchers
Rotary	Temple	Women's Clothing
Sales	Theater	YMCA
Scriptures	Title Company	Youth Baseball
Securities	Toastmasters	Youth Basketball
Security System	Trainer	Youth Football
Service	Training	YWCA
Service Organization	Transportation	Zig Ziglar
Service Station	Travel	

Appendix C

List of interesting Screen Names

If you find any name on this list appealing but it is being used by someone else, add a number or initials to the end of it. Make it unique to you and it's yours.

ABusinessCoach	CoachSteve	InvestmentQueen
ABusinessMentor	CyberCoach	JustMary
ACoach4You	CyberMentor	KnowledgeableAnn
ACoachForYou	DannySkyDiver	LadySuccess
AGlobalMentor	DavidTheDoctor	LarryTheBanker
AHomeBizCoach	DavidTheMentor	LarryTheLawyer
AMentor4Success	Denise4RealEstate	LifeBalanceMentor
AMentorForSuccess	DoctorDavid	LifeCoach4You
AmericanMentor	DoctorEFuture	LifeDesigner
AnnTheNurse	DoctorGoodSkin	LifestyleChanger
AnnuityKing	DoctorGoodTeeth	LifestyleCoach
ArthurTheSailor	DoctorSuccess	LifestyleCoach4U
ASailingMan	DownhillRacer	LifestyleDesigner
AStarMaker	DrFeelGood	LifestyleMentor
ASuccessCoach	DrGoodSkin	LivingMyDream
ASuccessfulMind	DrMakeWell	MannyTheSurfer
ASuccessGal	DrSuccess	MaryTheMentor
ASuccessGuide	eBizMentor	MaryTheNurse
ASuccessGuru	eBizMentorForYou	MasterOfSuccess
ASuccessMentor	eBusinessMentor	Mentor2Go
ATennisLover	FastCash4You	Mentor2U
AWonderMom	FlyBoyMark	Mentor2You
BaselineBobbie	FlyGirl777	Mentor411
BayouBob	GlobalCoach	Mentor4Freedom
BeachsideDiva	GlobalMentor	Mentor4Health
BlondeAmbition08	HenryTheMentor	Mentor4Lifestyle
BobbySkyDiver	HenryTheSailor	Mentor4Success
CaptainMike	HomeOnTheFarm	Mentor4Wealth
CaptainSuccess	InsightfulMary	Mentor911
Coach4U	InsuranceMan	MentorByTheBeach
Coach4You	InternetCoach	MentorForBeauty
CoachForYou	InternetMentor	MentorForHealth

MentorForSuccess	SailingHenry	TheLifestyleRealtor
MentorForU	SailorMan1	TheLitigator
MentorForWealth	SamTheSailor	TheLotMaven
MentorForYou	SeasideDiva	TheMeatMan
MentorMary	ShakleeForYou	TheRealEstateMan
MentorOnTheGo	SkatingGal	TheREspecialist
MentorToGo	SkinDoc2010	TheSailingMan
MentorToU	SnowBunny86	TheSolutionist
MentorToYou	StarMaker	TheStarMaker
MentorU4Success	Success2U	TheStockWiz
MikeTheGolfer	Success4U	TheStrikeKing
MillionaireMaker	SuccessBuilder	TheSuccessCoach
MiracleMaker	SuccessForU	TheSuccessFinder
MissPositive	SuccessForYou	TheSuccessGal
MissSuccess	SuccessfulGrandpa	TheSuccessGuide
MissWallStreet	SuccessfulMother	TheSuccessGuru
MisterSuccess	SuccessfulSally	TheSuccessLady
MovingToFlorida	SuccessGal	TheSuccessMaker
MrHomeBizCoach	SuccessGal1958	TheSuccessMan
MrHomeSuccess	SuccessGirl	TheSuccessMaster
MrPositive	SuccessHelper	TheSuccessMentor
MrSailorMan	SuccessMaker	TheSynergistUSA
MrsPositive	SuccessMentor	TheTennisAce
MrSuccess	SuccessMother	TheTicketFixer
MrTenPin	SuccessTutor	TownhouseGuru
MrWallStreet	SuccessWizard	TravelingMichael
MrWorkFromHome	SuzySkyDiver	UniversalMentor
MsAvidGolfer	TeacherAndMentor	USAMentor
MsBenefits	TennisLover	VirtualCoach
MsBlades	TheAdvocate	VirtualDeveloper
MsSuccessCoach	TheAvonLadyInTexas	VirtualFacilitator
MsTennis	TheBusinessCoach	VirtualInvestor
NancyTheGolfer	TheBusinessMentor	VirtualMentor
NestEggCreator	TheCyberMentor	VirtualStarMaker
NurseBetty	TheDeveloper	VirtualSuccess4U
NurseWithLapTop	TheFacilitator	WallStreetGuru
PoolLounger	TheGlobalMentor	WallStreetWiz
PoolsideDiva	TheInternetCoach	WeightLossMentor
PoolsideLounger	TheInternetMentor	WorldwideMentor
RealEstate911	TheInvestor	YourSuccessCoach
RightsProtector	TheLeadDog	YourSuccessTutor

Appendix D

List of common emoticons and Internet abbreviations

```
:-) . . . . . . . . . . . . . . . . . . . Smiley Face
:-( . . . . . . . . . . . . . . . . . . . Frowning Face
ASAP . . . . . . . . . . . . . . . . . As Soon As Possible
BBL . . . . . . . . . . . . . . . . . . Be Back Later
BBS . . . . . . . . . . . . . . . . . . Be Back Soon
BFN . . . . . . . . . . . . . . . . . . Bye For Now
BRB . . . . . . . . . . . . . . . . . . Be Right Back
BTW. . . . . . . . . . . . . . . . . . By The Way
C YA. . . . . . . . . . . . . . . . . . See Ya
GMTA. . . . . . . . . . . . . . . . . Great Minds Think Alike
HLOL . . . . . . . . . . . . . . . . . Hysterically Laughing Out Loud
HTH . . . . . . . . . . . . . . . . . . Hope This Helps
LOL . . . . . . . . . . . . . . . . . . Laughing Out Loud
LOLOL. . . . . . . . . . . . . . . . Laughing Out Loud On Line
MYOB . . . . . . . . . . . . . . . . Mind Your Own Business
NRN. . . . . . . . . . . . . . . . . . No Reply Necessary
OIC . . . . . . . . . . . . . . . . . . Oh I See
ROTFL. . . . . . . . . . . . . . . . Rolling On The Floor Laughing
TTFN . . . . . . . . . . . . . . . . . Ta Ta For Now
TTYL . . . . . . . . . . . . . . . . . Talk to you later
<vbg> . . . . . . . . . . . . . . . Very Big Grin
<g> . . . . . . . . . . . . . . . . Grin
<eg> . . . . . . . . . . . . . . . Evil Grin
<wg> . . . . . . . . . . . . . . . Wicked Grin
<-------- . . . . . . . . . . . . . Referring to yourself
<~~~~~ . . . . . . . . . . . . Referring to yourself
```

Appendix E

Helpful Resources

Audio CDs, Internet training programs, Your Daily Motivation by Max Steingart

If you're interested in taking your Instant Messaging activity to the next level after reading this book, you're going to want to visit my web site www.MaxSteingart.com to check out the most current Internet training courses available to you.

Shaking Hands on the Internet and Success Online

"Shaking Hands on the Internet" and "Success Online" are available in their 5th edition.

These two Internet training programs provide complete details on every aspect of Online friendship building, prospecting, recruiting, and increasing your customer base for any type of business.

They are an essential part of every sales person's Internet tool box and can be ordered online at www.MaxSteingart.com

Your Daily Motivation

Your Daily Motivation is a free service that is emailed to you every day. Sharing these messages is a wonderful and effective

way for everyone to stay in touch on a daily basis with their sales force, customers and new business prospects.

Everyone can use a positive daily reminder to jump start their day. The people in your Warm Market can read a thought-provoking message as soon as they turn on their computer each day, and think of you.

These messages will warm their hearts and inspire them. You will look forward to receiving them every day and you'll love the reaction you get from the people you send them to. They will have a profound impact on your life and the lives of everyone you share them with.

Your Daily Motivation inspires and uplifts the spirit of each recipient and raises their motivation level to new heights. These insightful messages have motivated people to start new careers and end others; start new relationships and abandon others; create greater goals and work harder to attain them, and so much more.

To receive Your Daily Motivation, visit www.YourDailyMotivation.com or www.MaxSteingart.com

Appendix F

Glossary

Address book
A useful Internet feature that permits you to store email addresses and other important information about the people you contact.

Blog
Derived from weblog, a blog is similar to an ongoing personal journal that is published on the World Wide Web. Many bloggers will allow anyone in the Online world to add their personal posting, creating an open forum on the web site. A wide range of subjects can be found on the growing number of blogging web sites. You can learn more at www.bloggers.com

Buddy List
Also called a contact list or messenger list, a Buddy List displays the screen names of your friends and family members who are Online when you're Online, allowing for easy, spontaneous Instant Message communication. You can add or remove people from your Buddy List at any time.

Chat
Conversational Hypertext Access Technology – 'talking' in real time over the Internet. To converse in an easy, familiar manner; talk lightly and casually. An informal, light conversation using Instant Messaging.

Chat Room
The name given to a place or page in a website or Online service where people can 'chat' with each other by typing messages which are displayed almost instantly on the screens of others who are in the Chat Room. Chat Rooms are also called 'Online forums.'

Community
A group of people having common interests. Similarities in identity. A community of interests. Sharing, participation and fellowship. See Online community.

Contact List
See Buddy List

Emoticons
Emotion + icon A Group of keyboard characters such as :-) typically representing a facial expression or an emotion or otherwise conveying tone or attitude that is used especially in computerized communications in Instant Messaging and email.

Etiquette
The practices and forms prescribed by social convention or by authority. Rules governing socially acceptable behavior. See Netiquette.

Friend
A favored companion; one attached to another by affection or esteem.

Innovation
The introduction of something new; a new idea or method.

Instant Message

Also abbreviated as IM. A convenient way to see when your friends and family are Online and communicate with them in real time. It's faster than email and more convenient than picking up the phone.

ISP

Internet Service Provider. An ISP is a company that provides access to the Internet.

Leader

One who leads or conducts; a person who has influence; a principal performer of a group; someone that has achieved a level of success. Someone that inspires others; a person whose success is an inspiration to others. Someone that helps others achieve success. No one wants to reinvent the wheel. Most self-help books written say to find someone that has been successful at the thing you want to achieve and do what they do.

Member Directory

A feature of an Instant Messaging system that permits all the users to publish personal profiles about themselves, that will be visible to everyone else using the system.

Messenger List

See Buddy List

Netiquette

Etiquette practiced or advocated in electronic communication over a computer network. It's a combination of the words network and etiquette and is an informal code of manners governing Online conduct. Netiquette can be as simple as not typing messages in all upper-case letters (this is interpreted as SHOUTING) or not spamming other Internet users and not posting commercial messages to newsgroups.

Networking
The exchange of information or services among individuals, groups or institutions; meeting people, making contacts exchanging ideas and interacting.

Network marketing
A term developed by members of the Direct Sales industry to describe a business model for moving products or services through the use of individual distributors or sales associates, used by over 44 million people around the world.

Online community
A group of people, Online, having common interests. While the entire global Internet is one Online community, the term is more specifically applied to particular interest groups, trades, cultural genres and local neighborhoods. There are hundreds of thousands of Online communities on the web.

Profile
The personal description of an Instant Messaging system user.

Relationship
A particular type of connection existing between people related to or having dealings with each other. A state of connectedness between people.

Screen Name
The name selected to identify an Instant Messaging system user.

Search Engine
A web site whose primary function is providing a searching mechanism for gathering and reporting information available on the Internet or a portion of the Internet.

SPAM
Unsolicited email, often of a commercial nature, sent indiscriminately to multiple mailing lists, individuals, or newsgroups; junk email. Also refers to inappropriate promotional or commercial postings to discussion groups or bulletin boards.

SPAMMING
SPAMMING is the practice of sending unsolicited bulk email.

SPIMMING
Acronym for 'SPAM Instant Messages.' Unsolicited real-time communication often of a commercial nature. See SPAM.

The Three Foot Rule – New
When you're sitting in front of your computer, you're within three feet of the entire Online world.

The Three Foot Rule – Old
When you're within three feet of a person that is breathing, they are a prospect for your business.

Virtual
Created, simulated, or carried on by means of a computer or computer network, i.e., virtual conversations in a Chat Room. Not real. The term virtual is popular in computer applications and is used in a wide variety of situations. In general, it

distinguishes something that is merely conceptual from something that has physical reality.

Warm Market
The people that you know

Your Daily Motivation
  Your Daily Motivation - free daily motivational messages written by Max Steingart. They are sent to you on a daily basis for you to share with your Online friends.
  See page 148 - Helpful Resources. To receive Your Daily Motivation go to www.YourDailyMotivation.com

About the author

Max is no stranger to introducing new computer applications. He has been helping people use computers to connect with other people since 1975, when he introduced an innovative computer system to the yacht brokerage industry. Money Magazine called him the "MatchMaker" because his computer generated lists made it easy for boat sellers to connect with people interested in buying a boat. Today, every major yacht brokerage firm in the world uses elements of a system he helped to create to conduct their business.

Max's innovative use of computers expanded beyond boats to other industries in the pre-Internet days. Airplanes, exotic automobiles, sport and luxury cars; thoroughbred horses, fine art, business opportunities and high-end real estate would all be added to his database. In 1989, Max was named the "Success Story of the Year" by Inc. Magazine for creating a company that was the forerunner of eBay..

AT&T called him a visionary in the computer industry.

Max has owned several successful businesses including the INC 500 publishing company previously mentioned. He's a highly quoted author, an innovative entrepreneur, and an entertaining lecturer.

Max has been a keynote speaker at many conferences and conventions. His Internet presentations have been described as entertaining, eye-opening, educational, and visually dazzling.

Since 1996, Max has been devoted to researching, studying, and developing a systematic method to teach people how to use the internet and Instant Messaging to network with other people.

In 1998, he introduced "The Perpetual Prospector," the first generic Internet training program for the Direct Sales Industry, followed two years later by "Success Online: Network Marketing in the New Millennium."

'Shaking Hands on the Internet' and 'Success Online: Relationship Marketing in the New Millennium' were initially published in 2002. Now available in the 5th Edition, they are an essential part of every sales person's Internet tool box. They can be ordered at his web site www.MaxSteingart.com

Max currently works directly with major corporations, home-based business owner groups, successful entrepreneurs and many direct sales companies. He is a contributing writer to many industry publications, a popular faculty member on most of the Online Internet training platforms, and has been a guest speaker on numerous radio programs. To schedule your own Online Tele-class or to have Max speak at your next event, email info@maxsteingart.com or call (204) 475-5245.

What people are saying about Max's trainings

"Max, I haven't seen anything that will impact my industry like your Internet training's since the introduction of video tapes back in 1988. I want everyone in my 80,000 plus organization to hear them. I've never recommended any generic training program that was developed outside my company until now."

Brent Bryson
Nu Skin - Big Planet, Salt Lake City, UT.

"Max, your program is the most comprehensive, foolproof prospecting training system ever developed. I predict it will take the network marketing industry to a whole new level of growth and prosperity."

Burke Hedges
Author - Who Stole the American Dream, Dream-Biz.com

"If you've ever wondered how you could use the Internet as a powerful prospecting tool, this is the book for you. Be prepared to have your paradigm changed. Max takes your through his system step by step with plenty of real world examples along the way. This is great information. Incredible Book!

Bob Burg
Author, Speaker, Trainer

Max Steingart is the master trainer of Recruiting on the Internet. He is the expert in the field. I am blessed to say that Max has agreed to partner up with us on a recruiting training Lab series that is unlike any other in the history of my business!

Doug Firebaugh
Chairman/CEO of PowerFire Training Group

What people are saying about Max's Tele-classes

To: Max Steingart
From: Betty Jean

Subject: The emailed responses we received from people about your Tele-class were wildly enthusiastic. I've enclosed a few of their comments. Can we schedule another call next month?

Sincerely
Betty Jean

AWESOME!! The energy on this call just comes through the phone and makes you want to hang up and start doing it!

Max Steingart is an exceptional mentor. His ability to teach his methods and techniques makes his course highly duplicatable through a downline which will result in massive success!

Clear, concise, gave very good examples. Kept my attention for whole hour. Has to be very good to do that.

He was great. Seemed committed to the success of the people on the call. Very generous with his time. Stayed on the call until there were no more questions.

Max is a great teacher and motivator. Would listen to him anytime.

Max was very enthusiastic and got right to the point of everything. He made everything easy to understand. I'm looking forward to listening to more of his classes.

MAKES YOU FEEL AS IF YOU ARE THE ONLY ONE HE IS TALKING TO. HE MAKES IT SOUND SO EASY.

GREAT INFORMATION ! RIGHT IN FRONT OF ME AND I DIDN'T SEE IT.

To see the current schedule of Max Steingart's Tele-classes visit:
www.maxsteingart.com